WALKING
on the
WATER
with
JESUS

ANTHONY J. RITTHALER

Clarke Books
Anna Maria Island, Florida

Also by Anthony J. Ritthaler
A Devil From The Beginning

Cover design, interior design, and eBook
by Blue Harvest Creative
www.blueharvestcreative.com

Walking on the Water with Jesus

Copyright © 2014 Anthony J. Ritthaler

All rights reserved. Except as permitted under the U.S. Copyright Act of 1976, no part of this publication may be reproduced, distributed, or transmitted in any form or by any means, or stored in a database or retrieval system, without prior written permission of the publisher.

Published by
Claʀke Books

ISBN-13: 978-1494995690
ISBN-10: 1494995697

Visit the publisher at:
www.clarkebooks.net

TABLE OF CONTENTS

INTRODUCTION

PSALMS 34:3: *O magnify the LORD with me,
and let us exalt his name together.*

COME ALONG WITH ME on a journey that you will never forget. Please allow me to take you through a tour of unbelievable scenes and outstanding wonders that God has performed in my life. I'm confident that these stories listed, in the pages to come, will excite, encourage and strengthen your faith in our Great Lord. If you're down in the valley, this book will lift your spirits in a wonderful way. I'm fully aware of the fact that people dwell in the midst of depression and despair more than ever in these last dark days, but God expects us to live with joy and peace on a daily basis. This book will give you hope and victory no matter what situation you find yourself in. My goal, in making these stories public, is to point you to Jesus Christ and not to feeble man. All the stories contained in this book are unexplainable with the human tongue and absolutely from God. When I study history, in great detail, I find that there are thousands upon thousands of Christians that have done far more than I have ever dreamed. Although most of these stories are from my own personal life, I will be the first to admit that God deserves all the glory for what he has done. Jesus said, in John (A) 12:32 that if I be lifted up from the earth, I will draw all men unto me. Please allow these stories to draw your eyes to the Savior and behold his glory in a wonderful way. You will be amazed by each and every story and I pray God will open your eyes like never before.

The bible teaches throughout His word, that we should not be ashamed of His goodness in our lives and we should spread the news to all mankind. Psalms (B) 107:2 says let the redeemed of the Lord say so. Psalms (C) 26:7 says that I may publish with the voice of thanksgiving, and tell of all thy wondrous works. Job (D) 19:23 says OH, that my words were now written, OH that they were printed in a book. Jesus said in Matthew (E) 5:16 to let your light so shine before men, that they may see your good works, and glorify your Father which is in heaven. God expects us to leave monuments, and memorials to the future generations so they can see the miracles that God performed in our lives. Many of the stories in this book remind me of Billy Sunday or D.L. Moody stories.

Get ready to be shocked, stunned and stirred as God is revealed in this book. The majority of the stories are positive and bright but some are serious and frightening. May God bless you as you read this project and I hope these stories will enlighten you in a brand new way?

JOHN 12:32: *And I, if I be lifted up from the earth, will draw all men unto me.*

PSALMS 107:2: *Hide not thy face from me in the day when I am in trouble; incline thine ear unto me: in the day when I call answer me speedily.*

PSALMS 26:7: *That I may publish with the voice of thanksgiving, and tell of all thy wondrous works.*

JOB 19:23: *Oh that my words were now written! Oh that they were printed in a book!*

MATTHEW 5:16: *Let your light so shine before men, that they may see your good works, and glorify your Father which is in heaven.*

ONE
THE NIGHT GOD OPENED A DOOR FOR ME

REVELATIONS 3:20: *Behold I stand at the door and knock:*

THE BIBLE TEACHES IN Revelations (A) 3:8 that God has set before us an open door which no man shutteth, and no man openeth. In John (B) 10:7 Jesus declares that I am the door. In other words God has the ability to open or close any door he chooses by the authority of the word of God. The story that I will now tell you is a real account which happened at my parents' house a few years ago. I am glad to report that Jesus is the same yesterday, today, and forever and He is still doing miracles today. Allow me to tell you a true story that is shocking to anyone who has ever heard it.

My wife and I decided to take a trip to my parents' house to pay them a visit on a Saturday night. It is always a joy to be around such godly people, who are always trying to grow in the things of God. I seem to learn something new when I'm in their presence and I have nothing but respect for my mom and dad. While we were fellowshipping and enjoying each other's company I looked at the clock and realized that it was already 12:30 a.m.and I still had to put my Sunday School lesson on paper for my teen class at church. I told my wife that I would get things ready and warm up the car. When I started the car I closed the door without noticing that the keys were inside and I accidentally hit the power lock button by mistake. Immediately I went to all four doors to check if they were all locked. Once I knew this was true I checked them for a second time hoping one would be opened. Reality then sunk in that I had made a foolish mistake, and now I must break the news to my wife.

As I walked in the house I couldn't believe what had just happened. I then walked into the living room to find that my family was all ready to leave. At this point all hope seemed gone and I figured this would be a long night. I then looked at my wife and told her the bad news. She couldn't believe it, and her response to me was, "You better find a way to get it open." When she made that remark I wondered just how this would happen.

As I went back outside the example about Peter in prison entered my mind. The bible declares, in Acts (C) 12:6-7 that God sent an angel and opened the prison for Peter, and I was praying He would do something for me. My first thought was go to the driver's side and check both doors to see if they were unlocked. After that didn't work I went to my daughter's door and I found that a miracle took place. Her door had opened and God helped me that night. I remember dancing for joy and running in the house at around 1:00 a.m. I told my wife that through prayer, God had opened Hopes door and we can go home now. Isn't it wonderful that we have a friend that sticketh closer than a brother? Glory to His name.

REVELATIONS 3:8: *I know thy works: behold, I have set before thee an open door, and no man can shut it: for thou hast a little strength, and hast kept my word, and hast not denied my name.*

JOHN 10: 7: *Then said Jesus unto them again, Verily, verily, I say unto you, I am the door of the sheep.*

ACTS 12:6: *And when Herod would have brought him forth, the same night Peter was sleeping between two soldiers, bound with two chains: and the keepers before the door kept the prison.*

7: *And, behold, the angel of the Lord came upon him, and a light shined in the prison: and he smote Peter on the side, and raised him up, saying, Arise up quickly. And his chains fell off from his hands.*

TWO

LIGHTNING STRIKING TWICE IN THE SAME YEAR

ROMANS 8:31: *What shall we then say to these things?*
If God be for us, who can be against us?

IF THIS CHAPTER DOESN'T prove God watches over our lives, then nothing will. When people hear these two stories it causes them to do some soul searching like never before. What I'm about to tell you seems impossible but it is true. It happened while at work one day, God opened the eyes of one of my co-workers in an outstanding way. Let me tell you what took place.

I work at Poco Inc., a company that supplies signs, barrels, barricades, and other equipment to companies around Michigan to help fix the roads. That day I was loading a barrel trailer for my company that was heading for Ann Arbor to repair a road in the area. While I was working I accidentally forgot that I put my keys on the side of the trailer. Without my noticing, the truck and trailer took off with my keys on the side of it. What's stunning about this is that the step on the side of the trailer is very small and there was nothing to hold my keys on it. When I finally was made aware that my keys were missing I began to look around the yard but I could not find them. I then notified my boss that my keys were lost and I may have left them on the trailer. My boss called Mark, the driver of the truck, and asked him to check if my keys were still on the trailer. At this point in the story, he had already been driving for over forty minutes on the highway going up and down hills and driving at speeds of 70 mph on his way to Ann Arbor. When he stopped the vehicle and looked he found my keys were still on the trailer where I left them. I still remember when Mark returned to the shop with my keys in his hand. He had a look on his face that was one of amazement. He dropped the keys on my bible and said to me, "Either I am a good driver or you're living right." I then replied, "It's probably a little bit of both." He walked away shaking his head and I thanked God for His goodness that day.

About six months later, lightning struck again, on a Sunday night. After church that night I strapped my little daughter, Hope, in her car seat for the ride home. However, I totally forgot that my bible was still on the trunk where I put it while I was putting Hope in her seat. My wife has a 2008 Chevy Cobalt with a trunk lid about the width of my bible. The car has no spoiler or anything that would hold my bible in place and it was pretty windy that night as we headed for the house. We drove about thirty minutes home and twenty of it was highway driving. I can still remember that at one point we were up to 80 mph and I quickly reduced my speed. When we arrived at our home in Canton, Michigan I went to get Hope out of her car seat and discovered my bible was still on the trunk, where I left it. The pages were blowing in the wind but it never moved an inch and nothing blew out of my bible. I'm still using that bible today.

God proves to me every day that without Him I can do nothing. The Lord always has His ever seeing eye open for His saints and these two stories prove it. What a wonderful God we serve!

THREE

THE POWERFUL GOSPEL TRUTH

ROMANS 1:16: *For I am not ashamed of the gospel of Christ: for it is the power of God unto salvation to every one that believeth; to the Jew first, and also to the Greek.*

THIS STORY, ABOVE ANY in this book, is my personal favorite because it involves the Word of God. Through the years, I have seen God's word do the unthinkable. Growing up with godly parents, with scriptures on the walls of their house, and God in their hearts, it is safe to say the bible has always been a big part of my life.

The bible, to me, is alive, vibrant, powerful, life changing, supernatural, and glorious all in one. The gospel story can still transform the lowest, darkest, vilest sinner and put him on a completely different path. My family and I have witnessed, first hand, just how far God's grace can reach. We have seen total drunks changed in a moment of time, drug addicts made brand new, and gang members choose a whole different path. There is no limit to the love of God, or the mercy that he is able to extend. It spoke to my heart, at a young age, and did something that nothing else has ever been able to do. It sliced and diced me to pieces, and saved me from the many heartaches that life throws at me. I still remember a story about God's word that will stir your heart about the gospel and reveal what it is capable of doing.

A teenager, who was listening to a preacher live on the internet from Israel, got under deep conviction of God about his soul while he was dangling his feet in the Jordan River. He told his parents that the Lord was dealing with his heart and his parents got on a plane with him and flew 9,000 miles to Tennessee, rented a car, drove one hour to where the preaching was taking place, and he cried out to God for mercy. The church rejoiced and was shocked that the gospel affected that young man so much. The bible teaches in Ephesians (A) 3:20 that God is able to do exceeding abundantly above all that we ask or think. It is an unstoppable force that convicts people's hearts and changes their future. Thank God for His Word that guides us through the pitfalls of life. Allow me to give you a story that still touches my heart to this day.

Around two years ago God began to deal with me about doing something special for a true man of God. It became very important to me, and I wanted to make sure the gift was perfect. Many of my ideas were good, but none were giving me peace about the situation. My dad then made a suggestion that finally gave me the peace I was praying about. He mentioned that 2011 was the 400th Anniversary of the first printing of the King James 1611 AD Bible and they were selling exact replicas on the Internet. It was all I needed to hear because there could not be a better gift, on planet earth, than that.

Although I desired that bible I promised my wife that we would not buy it unless we had the extra money. Sad to say, we didn't at the time, but I believed God was going to provide it, somehow. Three days later a miracle took place in the form of $1,048 dollars that dropped out of the sky. My wife's first words were to go ahead and get that bible you want. Joy overwhelmed my soul, and I was extremely grateful what God had done for me.

Without delay we ordered that bible and it cost $380 dollars. It weighed around 40 pounds and it was beyond explanation. Before I gave it to the man of God I wanted to take it around the country and find the best of the best Christians to sign it for him. Needless to say it involved much travel and deep thought but it was well worth it. These are some of the names I was able to capture; the great Squire Parsons, Doctor Lawrence Mendez, and Steve and Mary Earlywine missionaries to Mexico.

Brother Earlywine once told me that when he was in Mexico he went door to door on visitation for five hours a day, for nine years straight. Every person that signed this bible is very special in their own way. Some were amazing preachers, some were faithful missionaries, others were outstanding givers and the rest were examples that all could follow. I can still remember the reaction on people's faces when they saw that bible for the first time. My dad, for example, asked me if he could look at it for a while and he had a look of complete amazement, as he went through each page.

Brother Martin Cooke, of The Inspirations, had a response that I will never forget. Brother Cooke is the founder and pianist for the very famous Inspiration Quartet. Words cannot describe how faithful and precious he really is. For over 38 years The Inspirations have had a song that has made it to number one in the country, in the field of gospel music. As I asked Brother Martin Cooke if he would sign that bible he got very emotional. He then took the bible to a spot away from the crowd so he could view it for himself. After he was done signing the bible he thanked me and said that this bible is the most beautiful thing he had ever seen. Others wept and all had respect for God's glorious word. When I asked these wonderful people to sign the bible, I also had them write their favorite bible verses. Nearly everyone who signed the bible signed different verses from one another. The majority of the verses were from Psalms and Proverbs, but many also came from all over the Word of God.

One night, while at a Bob Evans Restaurant in Ohio, God swept over my soul in a special way. I leaned over and told my mother something that she and I will never forget. I told her that I was thinking of asking someone, in our church, to sign the bible and if he did I believe he would sign Hebrews (B) 4:12. To this day I can't explain why I said it but I knew God spoke to my heart that night. The next morning was a Sunday morning and this is the gospel truth. I approached the man who I was looking for, and he agreed to sign the bible for me. This man is very humble, quiet, and godly. Never, up to that point, had I ever seen him sign anything before but he did that day. As he took the pen and signed his name, I stood in amazement as he wrote Hebrews 4:12 as his verse.

After everyone signed the bible, he remained the only person to sign this verse. When I told my mom the story of how he signed the verse I said he would, she just couldn't believe it. In the King James Bible there are over 30, 600 verses contained in its pages. This man picked the exact verse I thought he would, and it still blows me away to this day. This will forever be a story that I can pass on for generations to come. The bible can be defined as Basic Instruction Before Leaving Earth. The bible still works just as good today, as it ever has. This personal example moves my heart every time I tell it.

EPHESIANS 3:20: *Now unto him that is able to do exceeding abundantly above all that we ask or think, according to the power that worketh in us.*

HEBREWS 4:12: *For the word of God is quick, and powerful, and sharper than any two-edged sword, piercing even to the dividing asunder of soul and spirit, and of the joints and marrow, and is a discerner of the thoughts and intents of the heart.*

FOUR
BLASPHEMING
THE HOLY SPIRIT

LUKE 4:18: *The Spirit of the Lord is upon me, because he hath anointed me to preach the gospel to the poor; he hath sent me to heal the brokenhearted, to preach deliverance to the captives and recovering of sight to the blind, to set at liberty them that are bruised.*

THE MOST DANGEROUS AND damnable subject in this entire universe is the subject we are covering in this chapter. Many will debate you, disagree with you, or even laugh at you when this subject is discussed in a public setting. Most Christians do not like to consider this subject so they would rather explain it away. I have heard people go to vast extremes to erase this biblical reality from people's minds. They do this through false teaching and human reasoning.

Years ago, in the fundamental movement, many preachers would warn sinners of the dangers of stepping over the line and blaspheming God's Holy Spirit. As a result, silence would fill the auditorium and the lost would run to the altar under Holy Ghost conviction. Many verses in the bible describe how God will destroy those who disrespect God's word. In the book of Proverbs alone there are multiple references that deal with disaster, sudden destruction, people's lamps being put out, and immediate death. Remember in 2 Kings (A) 2:23 where Elisha just received a double portion of the Spirit of God from Elijah. The bible records how little children met Elisha as he was going to Mt. Carmel from Bethel and decided that they were going to have fun at the man of God's expense. This decision proved to be fatal as Elisha cursed them in the name of the Lord. The word of God goes on to tell us that two she bears came out of the woods and killed forty-two of them for mocking the man of God. If I were to take you through God's Holy Word I would show you multiple times where God's anger was kindled against the lost for blaspheming His Holy Spirit.

In Matthew (B) 12:31-32: Jesus made a statement that should strike a dart of fear in an unbeliever's heart like nothing else can. His soul stirring words come at a point in His ministry when the crowds were thronging Him like never before. The Lord's fame was beyond belief and His miracles were beyond compare. Like the children in Elisha's day, the Pharisees in Jesus day made a foolish decision that grieved the Holy Spirit of God like nothing else in His three and a half year earthly ministry.

While Jesus was preaching and His Spirit was moving they accused the Lord of casting out devils by Beelzebub the prince of the devils. Their statement halted all the progress and wonderful blessings that others were witnessing at that present time. This caused the Lord to declare a statement that was stunning and earth shaking to those who were in attendance that day. Jesus turned to the Pharisees and uttered these fearful words. (B) 31 "Wherefore I say unto you, All manner of sin and blasphemy shall be forgiven unto men: but the blasphemy against the Holy Ghost shall not be forgiven unto men. 32 And whosoever speaketh a word against the Son of man, it shall be forgiven him: but whosoever speaketh against the Holy Ghost, it shall not be forgiven him, neither in this world, neither in the world to come."

In the book of Mark (C) 3:29 the bible proclaims, "but he that shall blaspheme against the Holy Ghost hath never forgiveness, but is in danger of eternal damnation." Notice Jesus said, at any given time, if a man speaks against the Son or the Father, he may be forgiven, but if a man speaks against His Spirit his chance of forgiveness is forever over. May I submit to you that John the Baptist was filled with the Holy Ghost from his mother's womb. David was a man after God's own heart and walked in the Spirit most of his life. Paul preached with power and thousands were touched through his amazing life. Jonah preached to Ninevah and the whole nation, even the beasts, repented and feared his message from God. Peter preached on the day of Pentecost and three thousand were saved. Jesus gave his Apostles power to turn the world upside down in Acts (D) 17:6. As a result people feared and respected God's men and God's word.

Jesus teaches us in His Holy Book that His Word and His Spirit are two things that should never be disrespected or taken lightly. God is very long suffering in all of our lives according to 2 Peter (E) 3:9 "The Lord is not slack concerning his promise, as some men count slackness; but is longsuffering to us-ward, not willing that any should perish, but that all should come to repentance." However, His long suffering becomes exhausted when the Lord's Spirit or His Word is blasphemed to a certain point.

Please allow me to explain what I mean. Dr. J Harold Smith, the great preacher who effected multitudes for the Savior, has one message that all should listen to. Dr. Smith preached a famous message entitled, "God's three deadlines." It is estimated that through that one message alone, over 1.4 million people have been converted to Christ. Dr. Smith describes, in great detail, this subject of blaspheming God's Holy Spirit. He said, in this message, that twenty-one times in is ministry he witnessed people blaspheming God's Spirit and God in return ended their lives within twenty-four hours; everytime. Dr. Smith lived as close to God as very few ever have. He would wake up at three in the morning, every day, and write a personal love letter to Jesus.

Dr. Smith lived so close to Jesus he knew nine years ahead of time the day he was going to die and he wrote it in his personal journal. Nine years later, the day he said he was going to die, was the day he went to heaven. Dr. Smith preached around seventy years reaching multitudes upon multitudes for Jesus. He preached live on radio and was faithful to his calling. In other words, he was a reliable source and someone you could take seriously.

God uses His word, preached by His men, filled with His Spirit to reach the lost. Where the Spirit of the Lord is, there is liberty, but when His Spirit is blasphemed, there is sudden destruction. Be very careful how you act when His Spirit is moving, because it could prove deadly in your life. God's Spirit is taken for granted in this generation, and as a result God will laugh at their calamity on judgement day.

The great Benjamin Franklin admitted that even though he was unconverted to Christ, he still had respect for George Whitfield. Mr. Whitfield, along with other men of that time, were responsible for something called The Great Awakening that can be found in your history books. During this short period of time, in America and other parts of the world, thousands upon thousands were saved through the efforts of the Mr. Whitfield. Strong conviction filled the land, and many lost people couldn't eat due to the fear of dropping off into hell. Mr. Franklin confessed that watching Whitfield preach was like nothing he had ever seen before. He calculated that one night, after leaving Mr. Whitfield's service and walking home, that this man of God could be heard from some three quarters of a mile away. Mr. Whitfield did not have the benefit of amplified sound, like we do, only God's Holy Spirit. When God's Spirit is present in the church it makes all the difference in the world.

Please allow me to give you an example from my life of someone who blasphemed God's Spirit and his life was abruptly ended. To this day I still tremble and shake whenever I think back on this incident, but I was there when it happened, so I guess I ought to know. I am humbled by the fact that before I left my twenties I witnessed this take place four times, with all of them people dying shortly after. I saw this take place four times in less than five years. God's Spirit is nothing to play around with and this account, when I was only twenty-six years old, is proof of that. Allow me to show you the severity of blaspheming God's Holy Spirit.

One day, while at work around five and a half years ago, I received word that my business had hired three new workers. My routine, at that time as it is now, was to welcome my new co-workers and ask if I could help them in anyway. I can honestly say, with my heart pure before God, that I have never judged anyone else that I have ever worked with because of their appearance or their bad habits. Who am I to judge anyone? Within my own heart lies the potential to be just as bad or worse than anyone I will ever meet. Jesus said in John (G) 15:5 "I am the vine, ye are the branches: He that abideth in me, and I in him, the same bringeth forth much fruit: for without me ye can do nothing." When I look at my own life, in light of the scriptures, I see a total mess without the grace and mercy of Almighty God.

With that being understood, for the first time in my life without knowing anything about a new man that started, God's

Spirit told me to keep my distance from him. Never before or never again has that ever happened to me, but I wanted to obey the Lord. Whenever he needed help I tried my best to help him, but I didn't go out of my way to seek him out like I did with everyone else. We later found out that he was stealing from everyone he could at work and buying drugs with it. He would tell us his daughter had cancer and needed help; while all the time using it for his own ungodly habit. I noticed that when he got around me he would want to talk about God, but everything he said seemed wrong in my soul. I found out later that when he was around others he would make fun of God and mock the bible.

One afternoon at work, a conversation took place between a fellow worker and myself that would prove fatal for this man. As I was working with a man named Jason something came out of my mouth that shocked both of us. At the time I knew very little about this man God told me to stay away from, but apparently the Spirit of God knew everything that I didn't know. I mentioned to Jason that I believe that this man I knew little about was going to die before the year was over and I don't know why. Jason said, "Why would you say that?" I said, "I don't know why but he will not live long." This man was quickly laid off from work and a few months went by without anyone hearing from him.

One day, while sitting in the break room talking to the guys, the Spirit of God swept over me and told me to open the bible immediately and at around 12:40 p.m. I opened my bible directly to Matthew (B) 12, without turning anywhere else. My eyes then fell on verses 31 and 32 where Jesus referred to blaspheming the Holy Ghost. I read both verses twice and closed my bible. A sudden quietness fell over me and I knew something was very wrong. For the next fifteen minutes I never said another word and people were asking if I was alright. I would just nod my head. My friend Tom Brown came to me, after lunch was over, and asked me if I remember this man who two months earlier I said would die. I responded that I did remember him and asked Tom, "What time did he die." Tom was in shock and he said, "How did you know he died?" I responded that God already told me around fifteen minutes ago.

Later in this book I will tell you a few more stories that relate to this topic and I pray that it will stir you like this one, no doubt, did. Please don't be an example, like this in someone else's book, respect the Lord for you are fearfully and wonderfully made. Psalms (H) 139:14 says, "I will praise thee; for I am fearfully and wonderfully made: marvelous are thy works; and that my soul knoweth right well." Always be careful how you live your life, the things you say or do can haunt you. A lost sinner once told a man of God, and I quote, "In life I wanted Him not, and in death He wants me not." Your tongue can liberate you or condemn you along life's road. It all depends on how you use it.

2 KINGS 2:23: *And he went up from thence unto Bethel: and as he was going up by the way, there came forth little children out of the city, and mocked him, and said unto him, Go up, thou bald head; go up, thou bald head.*

24: *And he turned back, and looked on them, and cursed them in the name of the LORD. And there came forth two she bears out of the wood, and tare forty and two children of them.*

MATTHEW 12:31: *Wherefore I say unto you, All manner of sin and blasphemy shall be forgiven unto men: but the blasphemy against the Holy Ghost shall not be forgiven unto men.*

32: *And whosoever speaketh a word against the Son of man, it shall be forgiven him: but whosoever speaketh against the Holy Ghost, it shall not be forgiven him, neither in this world, neither in the world to come.*

MARK 3:29: *But he that shall blaspheme against the Holy Ghost hath never forgiveness, but is in danger of eternal damnation:*

ACTS 17:6: *And when they found them not, they drew Jason and certain brethren unto the rulers of the city, crying, These that have turned the world upside down are come hither also.*

2 PETER 3:9: *The Lord is not slack concerning his promise, as some men count slackness; but is long-suffering to us-ward, not willing that any should perish, but that all should come to repentance.*

PROVERBS 1:26: *I also will laugh at your calamity; I will mock when your fear cometh.*

JOHN 15:5: *I am the vine, ye are the branches: He that abideth in me, and I in him, the same bringeth forth much fruit: for without me ye can do nothing.*

PSALMS 139:14: *I will praise thee; for I am fearfully and wonderfully made: marvelous are thy works; and that my soul knoweth right well.*

FIVE

GIVE AND YE SHALL RECEIVE

LUKE 6:38: *Give, and it shall be given unto you;
good measure, pressed down, and shaken together,
and running over, shall men give into your bosom.
For with the same measure that ye mete withal
it shall be measured to you again.*

THERE IS A SECRET within the blessed old book that few believe and claim as a promise in their own personal life. Whenever God makes a promise to us from His word it is a guarantee that it will come to pass. The bible says that "God cannot lie and that heaven and earth shall pass away, but my words shall not pass away." (A) The bible also says, "Let God be true and every man a liar." (B) The bible goes on to tell us that God is a debtor to no man and that God shall supply all our need. (C) In other words we can put full confidence in His word at all times.

In the Book of Luke 6:38, God makes a promise that if we give we shall receive. People all around the country doubt that this is true! They refuse to trust God with their funds and they limit the Holy One of Israel. Money has become a God to people and it has become a problem in the United States of America. If I took time to show you all the times God blessed me for giving by faith, and proved to me that Luke 6:38 was true, we would be literally using hundreds of examples. Please allow me to show you what I mean.

A young man got saved in our church and I could tell from the start that he was special. The Lord burned it in my heart to help him early and often. We attended a meeting in Detroit, Michigan one night and I had the joy of driving him to the inner city. As we began to talk I made it my goal that night to talk to him about this blessed subject. We talked about giving and receiving and the levels that it can take you with God. Many examples were given and the Spirit of God was moving in that car. I told him if he wanted to accomplish great things for the Lord he would have to help others along life's road. I then turned to the young man and made a statement that changed his life. I told him that if he determined to help others; God in return would do something special in his life. He told me he would do it and I knew he was telling the truth. Two weeks later, while working at Walmart, a fellow employee gave him a car for free. Things like that rarely happen but it did for him that day. What joy filled my heart when I heard the Good News.

Around a year later I had the joy of taking another young man under my wing. I tried to teach him the same truth. This man had a desire to do what was right and he became serious about giving. I made him the same promise and he took my advice. Around 2 days later he told me he helped just one person and a day later someone gave him a car that he is still driving today. Little is much when God is in it.

We have many examples in God's word that proves this is true. Remember how the lad gave Jesus his small lunch and Jesus took it and blessed it and fed 5,000 men, plus women and children. His disciples then took up 12 full baskets for themselves. Jesus proved that little is much when God is in it. I could go into many other examples from the bible with you but time would not allow it.

I stand amazed how God always gives back more than what we give out. Jesus knows my heart, and it is a heart of thankfulness for his mercy on me. I remember when God told me to give my 2000 Chevy S-10 pickup to a man of God one day while I was at my parent's house. I felt burdened about this thought and I was a little hesitant because I just recently paid my truck off. I was finally sitting good financially with no truck payment. When I made the decision to follow the Lord, and step out by faith, The Devil tried everything in his power to stop that from happening. The Devil had a plan but God had a bigger plan. The Lord allowed me to sell my truck for $4,000 dollars and immediately I went and got a cashier's check and sent it to Mississippi to the man of God. What I remember most about that experience was the moment I held that big check in my hand. The Devil quickly jumped on my Shoulder and whispered in my ear, "Do you really want to do that?" I realized, at that point, that $4,000 dollars is the most money I ever held in my hand at one time in my life. The bible teaches that we must trust God's word and not our feelings, and that is what I did.

It was a special feeling when that check left my hand and entered God's hand. At that time I had no back-up plan for another car, only God's promises. After a few days had past, God did something remarkable for me. While at my parent's house the Lord directed me to an ad in the paper displaying a 2005 Ford Mustang show car with only a few thousand miles on it. Basically, I was just looking because I knew I could never afford it. What's amazing about this is God reduced the price on that Mustang $4000 dollars which was the same amount I sold my truck for. God has everything thing under control in our lives if we can only follow his leadership. The preacher later told me that he had a special need at the time and his need was for $4,000 dollars to the penny.

The Mustang became a blessing to me and it was definitely an enjoyable ride. Every-where I went people gave me compliments on my beautiful car. A few years later God wanted to test my faith again, but this time it was with the Mustang. When the Lord spoke to my heart about giving my Mustang away to another preacher, I didn't know how to break the news to my wife. I told my wife that we needed to talk and she knew I was serious. The burden was heavy and my heart was over whelmed with joy as I told her what God put on my heart. She said OK it's your car and if God told you to do it then you should do it. Immediately after talking to my wife we talked to the preacher in private. He was almost speechless as he asked us to give him a day or two to talk with his wife about the situation. Two days later he made us a deal. He told us that the only way he would take the Mustang was if I took his car in return. We quickly agreed to that offer. The good Lord has blessed this move in a powerful way. Since that has happened, my mother offered me another car for free, the preacher gave me an expensive book for free and I no longer have a car payment.

Ever since we made this move in our lives, the windows of heaven have opened and on a daily basis God sends something our way. It has been remarkable to witness and it has been a joy to behold. Give and ye shall receive is more than a cute phrase, it is a biblical reality.

When giving is a part of your life, receiving will be as well. The first time I gave to the Lord it was hard for me, but as the years go by it has become easier and easier. Galations (D) 6:7 tells us that sowing and reaping is the eternal law of the harvest. If you sow good seed you will reap life eternal, but if you sow bad seed you will surely reap corruption in your life. It is really that simple!

MT: 24:35: *Heaven and earth shall pass away, but my words shall not pass away.*

ROM: 3:4: *God forbid: yea, let God be true, but every man a liar; as it is written, That thou mightest be justified in thy sayings, and mightest overcome when thou art judged.*

PHIL: 4:19: *But my God shall supply all your need according to his riches in glory by Christ Jesus.*

GALATIONS 6:7: *Be not deceived; God is not mocked: for whatsoever a man soweth, that shall he also reap.*

8: *For he that soweth to his flesh shall of the flesh reap corruption; but he that soweth to the Spirit shall of the Spirit reap life everlasting.*

SIX

THE GREAT BLESSINGS THAT COME WITH HELPING THE POOR

PROVERBS 22:2: *the rich and poor meet together:*
the LORD is the maker of them all.

THERE IS A SPECIAL place in the heart of God for the man or woman who will reach out for the less fortunate. There are many verses in the bible about helping the poor and needy. I believe the Lord is touched with the feelings of our infirmities and weeps over the pain we endure in our lives. Jesus' three and a half year ministry was full of examples of Him caring for the halt, lame, blind and the handicapped.

The bible declares, in 2 Corinthians (A) 8:9 that Jesus became poor that we may become rich. Jesus traveled from place to place, in his three and a half year earthly ministry without a home to call his own. He suffered hunger, thirst, felt pain, experienced hard times and He dealt with sorrow, just like we do. He always went after those who other people despised. He went after the woman at the well, the maniac of Gadara, and the demon possessed Mary. Jesus had a soft spot in His heart for the down and out of society and commands us to also care for sinners, no matter how bad they might be. Beyond all the tattoos, the scars, the bad history, and the past people carry around with them is a soul Jesus died for. I believe people miss out on major blessings, in their life, when they ignore the poor and pass up opportunities to be a help to someone in need. Every time you help a needy person through life God writes it down and remembers it in your future.

When I think of helping the poor and being blessed, my mind thinks about William Booth. Mr. Booth loved all mankind, but especially the poor. He gave his life to preach to the lost and bless the needy. God allowed him to start something called the Salvation Army. This outreach has spread worldwide and has helped millions through the years. Proverbs (B) 29:18 says where there is no vision the people perish. How you bless others will determine how much you will be blessed in the days to come.

My mind flashes back years ago when I had the joy of helping a very poor woman in buying her a car. This car was instrumental in bringing her family to church for around 7 years. It brought joy to my heart that this world can not give. I felt like I made a real difference that day and God blessed me for it. The very next day after I bought that woman a car, my boss told me that I would have a pay increase on my next check. God always blesses those who help the poor. I'm going to tell you two stories of how beneficial it is to help the poor and Lord willing it will motivate you to do it. I Timothy (C) 6:7 tells us that we brought nothing into this world and it is certain we can carry nothing out. The only thing that's going to matter, when we die, is what we did for Jesus. Let these two stories speak to your heart as you read them.

There was a famous preacher that decided one day to help a very troubled and needy child that had come to his church. The boy had a rough past and not even his parents showed interest in his future. He had no friends to speak of and no one that loved him. The preacher's heart ached for that boy and he was the only person on earth that was willing to offer any help towards him. He took the boy under his wing and started to see progress as the young man was growing. One day the pastor went to check on him and found that the young man had vanished from his place and ran away. The pastor searched for the boy but he could not be found. Many years later, on a Sunday morning, a visitor showed up in a new suit, a new tie, and brand new shoes. When the offering was given this man calmly dropped a check in the plate for one million dollars and addressed it, "For the Preacher." After service the Pastor went to the man and thanked him for such a kind offering that day. When the Pastor got a closer look at the man he realized that it was the boy he loved when nobody else would. He became a millionaire and he wanted to repay the love that the preacher showed him when he was a little boy.

Sometimes, when you help the poor, God will bless you in a way that is staggering years down the road. Psalms (D) 41:1 says "blessed is he that considereth the poor; the Lord will deliver him in time of trouble."

The second story that I pray will speak to your heart is one from my own life at a gas station a few years ago. Nearly every chance I get, and God knows my heart, I try to extend a hand of mercy to the poor. On the other hand I really try my best to use wisdom in each and every situation I encounter. The word of God says that if a man don't work he shouldn't eat. Fully capable, healthy people that refuse to work have no reason, according to the bible, to beg from those who work. God says in Proverbs (E) 20:4 that the sluggard will not plow by reason of the cold; therefore shall he beg in harvest and have nothing. God always condemns laziness and has ordained that we work with our hands and provide for ourselves. The Lord tells us in I Timothy (F) 5:8 but if any provide not for his own, and especially for those of his own house, he hath denied the faith, and is worse than an infidel. There are people out there that are smooth talkers and quick thinkers when it comes to stealing your hard-earned money, and you need to be careful. A man approached me one day and said he knew me and needed some money. He told me that he worked with me but couldn't remember my name. I found out later that he told the owner of the store I was at that he was his next door neighbor in Livonia, Michigan but the owner never lived in Livonia. People will go to any extreme necessary to trick you so they can fulfil their ungodly agenda. Every situation requires discernment and wisdom on our part because there are thousands of people that really do need help.

Let me tell you this story and I hope it helps you. One day, late at night, I pulled into a gas station and I saw a man digging in the garbage can for bottles. As I watched this man for a moment something told me to help him in any way I could. I reached behind my seat and found a pop bottle and gave it to the man. He thanked me over and over for that one pop bottle and I could tell he meant it. Verses about helping the poor raced through my mind and as he walked away my heart broke. I remember chasing him down and giving him another bottle and the only two dollars in my wallet. A tear came to his eye and my heart was instantly healed. The next day, at work, they asked me to go on the road and help close a freeway. I rarely get a chance to go on the road and make state wages but after I helped that poor man God gave me an extra $200.00 that day. I am convinced it is because I helped the poor the day before.

The bible teaches us in Ephesians (G) 4: 32 that we ought to be tenderhearted forgiving one another even as God for Christ sake hath forgiven you. Ask yourself, when was the last time I helped someone in need. You may find that the answer will surprise you. The bible still teaches whoso stoppeth his ears at the cry of the poor; he also shall cry himself but shall not be heard. Proverbs (H) 21:13

2 CORINTHIANS 8:9: *For ye know the grace of our Lord Jesus Christ, that, though he was rich, yet for your sakes he became poor, that ye through his poverty might be rich.*

PROVERBS 29:18: *where there is no vision, the people perish: but he that keepeth the law, happy is he. Says where there is no vision the people perish.*

I TIMOTHY 6:7: *for we brought nothing into this world, and it is certain we can carry nothing out.*

PSALMS 41:1: *blessed is he that considereth the poor: the LORD will deliver him in time of trouble.*

PROVERBS 20:4: *The sluggard will not plow by reason of the cold; therefore shall he beg in harvest, and have nothing.*

I TIMOTHY 5:8: *But if any provide not for his own, and especially for those of his own house, he hath denied the faith, and is worse than an infidel.*

EPHESIANS 4:32: *And be ye kind one to another, tenderhearted, forgiving one another, even as God for Christ's sake hath forgiven you.*

PROVERBS 21:13: *whoso stoppeth his ears at the cry of the poor, he also shall cry himself but shall not be heard.*

SEVEN

PROOF THAT GOD GIVES US THE DESIRES OF OUR HEARTS
(THE HERSHEY BAR STORY)

PSALMS 37:4: *Delight thyself also in the LORD; and he shall give thee the desires of thine heart.*

THIS STORY, IN PARTICULAR, shocks more people than any other story that I will tell in this book. The detail and the amazement of this story puzzles people to this day. When I describe this event in my life, I still find it hard to believe. The bible says in Romans (A) 8:28 "And we know that all things work together for good to them that love God, to them who are the called according to his purpose." When you walk by faith and not by sight anything is possible with the Lord. Jesus said in Matthew (B) 17:20 "If ye have faith as a grain of mustard seed, ye shall say unto this mountain, remove hence to yonder place; and it shall remove; and nothing shall be impossible unto you."

The average Christian spends the majority of their time doubting God and therefore miracles are only things they read about, but it is not a reality in their everyday walk with God. The bible says in 1 John (C) 5:14-15 "And this is the confidence that we have in him that, if we ask any thing according to his will, he heareth us." 15: "And if we know that he hear us, whatsoever we ask, we know that we have the petitions that we desired of him." When you pray you must believe God will answer you according to His will. The great George Mueller had around 30,000 answers to prayer throughout his life and they were all in private. Let me tell you this amazing story that has become a reality for me.

Around a year ago, in the summer time, God put something unusual on my heart that I wanted to get a preacher. It was so unusual that I really had to make sure it was God's will and not my own thoughts. After a few days of making it a matter of prayer I told my wife that I believe God was going to put it in someone's heart to buy me a five-pound Hershey bar to give to a preacher. Her first reaction was like Sarah when she found out that she would have a baby at ninety years of age. My wife thought it was crazy, to be honest, I did too, but I was sure God spoke to my heart. Week after week passed and still no sign of a five-pound Hershey bar. As time passed on my faith never wavered because I was confident God spoke to me.

One day, while reading the bible at work, a young man named Steve shouted across the breakroom, in my direction, and from then on a glorious conversation took place. He said," Tony, do you know what I'm going to get you when I get some money?" I said," What's that Steve?" He said," A five pound Hershey bar; have you ever seen one?" My heart skipped a beat as I replied," I sure have." Little did he know that I had been praying about that for months. God is a faithful God that answers our requests like in days of old. When you think about how rare that was it almost seems like the stars were aligned at exactly the right time for that to happen. You see, His thoughts are not our thoughts, neither is His ways our ways. God works in a totally different way than we do. Jesus knows the beginning from the end and the hairs on our head are all numbered. When God did that for me it strengthened my faith and blessed my soul.

Do you know that ever since that day two other people also offered me a five pound Hershey bar and a teenager bought me a one pound Hershey bar for Christmas? Also, since that day God has put it on the heart of people that I work with to buy bulk candy with small Hershey bars in it. They tell me everyday to help myself. If anyone can explain how God did that, please let me know. Mark (D) 6:6: And he marveled because of their unbelief. And he went round about the villages, teaching. How much do we believe God, and how much more could He possibly do to convince us.

ROMANS 8:28: *And we know that all things work together for good to them that love God, to them who are the called according to his purpose.*

MATTHEW 17:20: *And Jesus said unto them, Because of your unbelief: for verily I say unto you, If ye have faith as a grain of mustard seed, ye shall say unto this mountain, Remove hence to yonder place; and it shall remove; and nothing shall be impossible unto you.*

I JOHN 5:14: *And this is the confidence that we have in him, that, if we ask any thing according to his will, he heareth us: 15: And if we know that he hear us, whatsoever we ask, we know that we have the petitions that we desired of him.*

MARK 6:6: *And he marveled because of their unbelief. And he went round about the villages, teaching.*

EIGHT

THE DAY GOD
SENT AN ANGEL MY WAY

HEBREWS 13:2: *Be not forgetful to entertain strangers:*
for thereby some have entertained angels unawares.

AS I READ THROUGH the word of God I quickly realize
that angels cover the pages of the Holy Scriptures. Hebrews
(A) 12:22 tells us that there are an innumerable company of
angels. Psalms (B) 34:7 talks about how the angels of God
encampeth around them that fear Him. Remember how
Gabriel appeared before Zacharias showing him that his wife
Elizabeth would soon have John the Baptist who would be
great in the sight of God. Or recall when an angel of the Lord
appeared unto Samson's mother to announce that she would
conceive and give birth to a man child that would judge Israel
for twenty years.

I often think about how Jesus told the world, in Matthew
(C) 26:53 that He had the ability to call twelve legions of angels
to deliver Him from the cross if need be. The bible also says
that they excel in strength according to Psalms (D) 103:20. The
bible teaches that they protect his saints in the book of Daniel
(E) 6:22. Angels have many different abilities and purposes

found in the bible. If I expounded on them it would surely take up the rest of this book.

In my thirty years of being in church and hearing hundreds of good men of God preach, I have never once heard a preacher cover this topic in a service. My thoughts on why I never have are probably because many people are afraid to teach on the spirit world because it is somewhat unknown. People are unsure on the subject of demons and angels so they deny it all together. With that being said it does not change the reality of the battle between light and darkness as we know it. I refuse to lie to myself about angels and dare not change the truth of God's written word. The story I'm about to tell you is as real as the paper that I am writing on, and it should make your heart skip a beat.

Many years ago, while at work, something happened that sticks with me until this very day. That morning it was very busy and fast pace. I remember working at an incredible rate and going up to receive another order to complete when all of the sudden I was approached by a total stranger. When I asked him if he needed help with anything he responded in an unusual way. He called me by my first name. I was shocked that he knew my name seeing that we had never met before. He went on to ask me if I knew where the verse was, in the bible, about strength. Not really understanding the importance of what was taking place I told him the verse he was looking for was Philippians (F) 4:13. That verse tells the believer that we can do all things through Christ which strengtheneth me. He then responded by saying, "Thank you Tony"and walked away. To this day I never caught his name, but he sure knew mine.

When looking back on this incident I stand amazed that the Savior would send an angel my way. This moment in time changed my mindset concerning angels. Thanks be unto God for his watch care over us.

Many other times throughout my life I have felt the presence of angels and unknown forces keeping me safe. The Lord knows I am humbled for his hand of safety on my life. When we get to heaven and God gives us perfect understanding, only then will we comprehend His love toward us. When you study God's word, notice how many times it refers to His love and protection towards the Christian. You will then have a new found respect for God's mercy like never before. Angels are all around us, at all times. If we keep that in mind, it will help us walk the strait and narrow way for the Master.

HEBREWS 12:22 *But ye are come unto mount Sion, and unto the city of the living God, the heavenly Jerusalem, and to an innumerable company of angels.*

PSALMS 34:7 *The angel of the LORD encampeth round about them that fear him, and delivereth them.*

MATTHEW 26:53 *Thinkest thou that I cannot now pray to my Father, and he shall presently give me more than twelve legions of angels?*

PSALMS 103:20 *Bless the LORD, ye his angels, that excel in strength, that do his commandments, hearkening unto the voice of his word.*

DANIEL 6:22 *My God hath sent his angel, and hath shut the lions' mouths, that they have not hurt me: forasmuch as before him innocency was found in me; and also before thee, O king, have I done no hurt.*

PHILIPPIANS 4:13 *I can do all things through Christ which strengtheneth me.*

NINE

THE LORD LISTENS TO OUR CRY FOR HELP

MATTHEW 15:22: *And, behold, a woman of Canaan came out of the same coasts, and cried unto him, saying, have mercy on me, O Lord, thou Son of David; my daughter is grievously vexed with a devil.*

THE GREAT DR. PHIL Kidd has a saying and I quote, "When hope is all gone; help is on the way." God has a way of showing up when life has reached its lowest possible level. The bible teaches, in Hebrews (A) 7:25, that God is able to save them to the uttermost that come to him. No matter how sinful a man or woman lives the blood of Jesus can cover any transgression ever committed. Story after story throughout the pages of time reveal the fact that God came to seek and to save that which was lost (Luke (B) 19:10) Sometimes the Lord must bring a man to his breaking point before he will seek the help that he so badly needs. From Charlotte Elliot, who wrote *Just As I Am* to William Cowper, who wrote *There Is A Fountain Filled With Blood* God has a way of getting one's attention and drawing them by His wonderful grace.

In this chapter I will give you two stories from my life where God showed up, in gloomy situations, to answer a few cries for help. Both situations are different, but both are powerful in their own way. I trust that God will help you through these two stories and prove to you that he is still on His throne and He still answers prayer.

One day, as I was spending time with my family, the phone rang and a woman was on the other end of the phone begging for prayer. She told me that she was desperately in need of a job and she hadn't worked in eight months. This woman went on to say that she had put in fifty applications without one single response. She asked me to pray for her about a certain job that she desired and I promised her I would. The very next day the same lady called me with a joy that was not there the day before. She told me that the very next morning, after we talked, a company called her about a job. After eight months of searching it only took one night of prayer to get her a job. She also told me that out of the fifty job applications she applied for she got the certain job that we prayed about. The bible tells us, in Psalms (C) 86:10, "For thou art great, and doest wondrous things: thou art God alone." It is such a blessing to know that God hears the prayers of His saints and moves on our behalf.

The second story I wish to share with you is a little more serious and is very amazing. One night, at church about 7:10 p.m., a woman I work with suddenly came to my mind and my soul was troubled for her. It seemed like she needed help and God wanted me to put her on the church's prayer list immediately. My heart became burdened for her that night and I remember loosing a little sleep thinking about if she was O.K. The next morning at work this same woman approached me with a broken spirit and tears running down her face. She told me that she tried to find my number but couldn't and at around 7:10 p.m. she almost took her life, but something stopped her from doing it. I told her that it was God who stopped her, and that I was praying for her at that exact moment. After we talked for a minute or two the Spirit of God spoke to my heart about giving her a preaching CD that could help her if she would listen to it. Although I have hundreds of preaching CD's, God told me to give her one entitled, *Manifestations of Demonic Activities*. It is a CD about the crazy man from Mark chapter 5. This man was crying and cutting himself with stones and lived day and night in spiritual bondage. The bible tells us that no one was willing to help him because he was seemingly a hopeless case. The community would just pass by him everytime. Often he tried to end it all and felt, within himself, that no one cared for his soul. When his life was at its lowest possible point and no one seemed to show interest in this man, thank God Jesus showed up at the perfect time to offer him hope.

Mark chapter 5 also tells us that this crazy man ran to Jesus and found the peace that he was looking for his whole life. My prayer in giving her this CD was that she would listen to it, fall under conviction, and run to Jesus for help like the crazy man did in Mark chapter 5. The Lord answered my prayer and the floodgates opened in this young lady's life. The next day, after I said that prayer, she told me that she listened to that CD I gave her 4 times. She promised to be at church Sunday to hear the gospel story. My heart was overwhelmed with excitement and I could see the spirit of God working on this young lady. The following Sunday she kept her promise and attended the house of God. She sat in the back that morning but God turned the altar into a magnet and brought her to the front at invitation time. Out of all the subjects that the preacher could have preached from that day he chose to preach from Mark chapter 5. My mother helped lead her to Christ that morning and our church shouted the victory.

God is still in the soul saving business and burdens can still be lifted at Calvary. Run to Christ while He is passing by and you too can be seated, clothed and in your right mind all the days of your life.

HEBREWS 7:25: *Wherefore he is able also to save them to the uttermost that come   unto God by him, seeing he ever liveth to make intercession for them.*

LUKE 19:10: *For the Son of man is come to seek and to save that which was lost.*

PSALMS 86:10: *For thou art great, and doest wondrous things: thou art God alone.*

TEN
GOD MOVING
ON MY BEHALF

HEBREWS 11:6: *But without faith it is impossible to please him: for he that cometh to God must believe that he is, and that he is a rewarder of them that diligently seek him.*

WHEN I THINK ABOUT the opportunity we have to help others, it really touches my heart in a special way. God says in II Corinthians (A) 9:7 "Every man according as he purposeth in his heart, so let him give, not grudgingly, or of necessity: *for God loveth a cheerful giver.*" He loveth a cheerful giver and He wants us to be a servant to others. The book of Jude (B) verse 22: says, "and of some have compassion, making a difference.." When we help others I am convinced that God smiles and is happy with that decision.

The word of God teaches that we should become a living sacrifice, (Romans (C) 12:1) on a daily basis, if we want His blessings in our lives. Sad to say that a very small percentage of Christians take that verse of scripture to heart and it stops them from many blessings they could enjoy. Every day of my life I've determined to help others because that's what it's all about. I believe that sowing good seed, throughout your life, will produce a harvest of positive things on a daily basis. When you give, with a pure heart, God in heaven will remember and reward that act of kindness in due time. Let me give you a story, from my life, that proves this is true.

Something that makes me very proud, in my life, is the decision I made years ago about helping at least one person every day. For eleven years, without fail, the good Lord has used me to help someone every day. This glorious decision in my life has produced a joy that this world could never give. For years and years I would give and it seemed like people would never give back. For around seven years this trend continued until one wonderful day God showed up when I needed him most. It was a long, hot summer day with the heat reaching dangerous levels at work. I was on the verge of passing out and to say I was thirsty was an under statement. We were not allowed to leave, after lunch was over, to go to the store and I was out of money. I remember saying a quick prayer to God asking Him for a drink of some sort. Within ten seconds my boss came through the door and said, "Tony, can I buy you a drink today?" I replied, "Yes, Sir!; and thank you very much." It was awesome how quick God answered that prayer. About thirty seconds after my prayer was answered another man came in the building and asked me if he could buy me a drink because something told him he should. I told him, "No thanks, someone just did but I appreciate the gesture." Before that day, I could not recall one time where someone offered me one thing at work but that day two people did in less than a minute.

It is a great feeling to know that God is with us when we need Him the most. Never stop helping others because that will be the day when God stops helping you. You will find that in life if you put Jesus first, others second and yourself last it will always produce JOY in your walk with God.

II CORINTHIANS 9:7: *Every man according as he purposeth in his heart, so let him give; not grudgingly, or of necessity: for God loveth a cheerful giver.*

JUDE VS 22: *says, "and of some have compassion, making a difference."*

C. ROMANS 12:1 *I beseech you therefore, brethren, by the mercies of God, that ye present your bodies a living sacrifice, holy, acceptable unto God, which is your reasonable service.*

ELEVEN

HEARING GOD'S VOICE

HEBREWS 3:15: *While it is said, Today if ye will hear his voice, harden not your hearts, as in the provocation.*

THE BIGGEST PROBLEM FACING Christians in this day and age is their inability to get alone with God. The average Christian surrounds himself with loud music, large crowds, dark atmospheres and bad influences. This produces much confusion, no peace, and bad choices in their lives. The ability to hear God in all this madness disappears and this results in sinful acts that destroy their future for God.

Christians today get caught up with this fast pace society and adapt the habits of a godless world. Between television, Internet, cell phones, work, school and raising a family, people's time is completely consumed and the Lord is forgotten. Christians have replaced songs like "Softly and Tenderly" with Christian rock and Christian rap. Their life is controlled by activities, fun time, stress and selfishness. Most people spend more time brushing their teeth and letting the dog out than they do thinking about God.

In I Kings (A) 19:12 God spoke to Elijah with a still, small voice and Elijah had the ability to hear it. Most Christians today wouldn't have heard the voice because they live such a carnal, wicked, and uncommitted life. God longs to have fellowship with his children but we hinder Him through our life style and are unable to hear Him speak to our hearts. Often, in the bible, Jesus went into the mountains all night praying to the Father. Daniel prayed three times a day and John the Baptist was alone learning from God. John the Beloved wrote the Book of Revelation while he was alone on the Isle of Patmos. Jesus wants us to be swift to hear, slow to speak and slow to wrath (James (B) 1:19).

We must have "alone time" with God so we can be in a position to hear His voice when He speaks to our hearts. Ever since I was a child I have tried my best to stay unspotted by the world and to get alone with Jesus. Never, in my life, have I consumed alcohol or smoked cigarettes. I have never been at a party or ran with the wrong crowd. Never have I listened to loud music or attended fun night at school. Like David, I hate sin and anything that resembles it. Though I fail God, I'm sorry when I make mistakes and listen to as much preaching as possible. These decisions, in my life, have allowed me to stay in a position to hear God's voice when he speaks to my soul. This has produced great joy and unbelievable blessings that only come when God is directing our lives.

One of the best decisions I ever made in my life was when I decided to purchase one hundred and forty preaching tapes at Christmas one year. During a two-month period I listened to all one hundred and forty preaching tapes and never said one word. God gave me much knowledge through that experience and helped me grow as a Christian.

In my opinion, hearing others, without interjecting our own beliefs, is a gift from God. The Lord gave us two ears and one mouth for a reason. We must train ourselves to learn from others every chance we get. Romans (C) 10:17 says that faith cometh by hearing and hearing by the word of God. Proverbs (D) 1:5 says a wise man will hear and increase learning. When we get to the point where we feel we have arrived, and disregard others wisdom, we will stop growing as a Christian. II Peter (E) 3:18 says "But grow in grace, and in the knowledge of our Lord and Saviour Jesus Christ." We need to find time to get alone with God multiple times each day.

In this chapter we will look at a few times when God spoke to my heart, in a clear way, and used me to bless others. Through these examples you will see how important it is to hear God's voice and follow His leadership. These examples will prove that God still speaks to hearts today and I pray they will motivate you to get closer to God each and every day.

Many years ago, while sitting in my truck at work, God spoke to my heart in a way that was direct and clear. He told me to write a check for $1,500 dollars and give it to a man of God in Detroit. This pastor was dear to my heart but $1,500 dollars was a lot of money at that time for me to sign over. After a few minutes of thinking it over I remember taking my checkbook out and writing him that check. When I signed my name and put it in my bible I felt a wonderful peace come over me and the Glory of God filled my truck. Words cannot express the feeling I had on the inside and I couldn't wait for church to arrive so I could give him that monster check. When I made it to church that following day, joy filled my soul as I gave him that check in private. As he looked at the check he asked me if I was sure I wanted to do this. I said in response that God spoke to my heart and told me to do it. He then pulled out a dentist bill that he had and said, "Look at the total on the bill." When I looked at the bill I saw that he had two teeth pulled and it cost him exactly $1,500 dollars. When God speaks to your heart, respond to Him with faith and assurance like I did that day and God will bless you.

The second story that comes to my mind happened a few years back at Hope Baptist Church. While sitting in church one day, listening to the message on a Sunday night, God told me to give a new couple in the church $100 dollars. After service I wrote a check for that amount and gave it to them in the parking lot before they left. When I told them God wanted me to give them that check for $100 dollars tears filled their eyes as they thanked me for the money. A few weeks later the man I helped told me that check was an answer to prayer and he wanted to tell me a story. He went on to say that before church that night he and his wife received a bill that day for $100 dollars and they didn't get paid until the next Friday. In the parking lot, before church that night, they asked God to send the money and help them in their time of need. God used me to meet their need and both the couple and I shouted the victory that day.

The third story I will share with you took place at work while I was reading my bible at lunch. That particular day I packed a light lunch and I was hungry. Near the end of my reading, at around 12:50 p.m. in the afternoon, I came to Psalms (F) 146:7 which says that God giveth food to the hungry. My eyes seemed to gaze on those words and I looked at that verse a number of times. God spoke to my heart at 12:55 p.m. and told me that He was going to prove that verse to me and give me some food that day. Within twenty minutes, of God speaking to my heart, three different people offered me food that day. I have learned over the years that God moves in mysterious ways, and that He can do the impossible if we will only hear His voice.

The final story I want to give you also took place at work and it will speak to your soul. As I was reading God's word one day the Lord told me to buy a candy bar and hand it out to someone. Immediately I rose from my seat and obeyed the voice of God. As I went to the machine to buy a Milky Way, a man came in the building and said, "What do you need, Tony?" I said to him, "What do you mean by that statement?" He said to me, "You must need something because something told me to come in here and give you some candy." He opened his bag and said, "Take anything you want." The bible says in Luke (G) 6:38 give and ye shall receive. God can give you anything you desire if you will listen to His voice and do what he commands you to do. Jesus said in John (H) 10:27 "My sheep hear my voice, and I know them, and they follow me." The more you obey God's voice the more you will have life, and have it more abundantly.

God is searching for those who will make Him the center of their lives and communicate with Him on a regular basis. When is the last time you heard his voice in your life?

I KINGS 19:12: *And after the earthquake a fire; but the LORD was not in the fire: and after the fire a still small voice.*

JAMES 1:19: *Wherefore, my beloved brethren, let every man be swift to hear, slow to speak, slow to wrath.*

ROMANS 10:17: *So then faith cometh by hearing, and hearing by the word of God.*

PROVERBS 1:5: *A wise man will hear, and will increase learning; and a man of understanding shall attain unto wise counsels: says a wise man will hear and increase learning.*

II PETER 3:18: *But grow in grace, and in the knowledge of our Lord and Saviour Jesus Christ. To him be glory both now and for ever. Amen.*

PSALMS 146:7: *Which executeth judgment for the oppressed: which giveth food to the hungry.*

LUKE 6:3:8 *Give, and it shall be given unto you; good measure, pressed down, and shaken together, and running over, shall men give into your bosom. For with the same measure that ye mete withal it shall be measured to you again.*

JOHN(H) 10:27: *My sheep hear my voice, and I know them, and they follow me.*

TWELVE

THE AMAZING TOOTSIE ROLL STORY

PSALMS 126:3: *The LORD hath done great things for us; whereof we are glad.*

THE STORY I'M ABOUT to tell you shocks and amazes everyone that hears it. When I think back on this story I must confess that it still staggers my thinking as well. The details and events that lead to this blessing are still hard to believe. Let me tell you the story and show you that the goodness of God will lead men to repentance.

When my daughter was around one year of age, we happened to be walking through Meijer around the time of Thanksgiving. The store was all decorated for the holidays and they had everything already setup. When you first walked into Meijer you would have certain displays that would instantly catch your eye. My daughter was fascinated with fish, at the time, and she kept pointing to the back of the store where they were located. On our way to the fish something caught my eye long before we got there.

Immediately, when I stepped into the store, I saw a large amount of rare candy that got my attention. You see, I like candy, any kind of sweets. That display got a hold of me for the rest of the night. The first item I saw was a gigantic Reese Cup that must have been a half pound. I had seen it before so it wasn't a big deal to me. The second thing I saw was a five-pound Hershey Bar that seemed bigger than life and was simply awesome to behold; however I must admit that I had seen them in days gone by as well. The last item I looked at was something that was a first for me. It was to become a special part of my life. What I saw was the biggest Tootsie Roll that I had ever laid my eyes upon.

Something about that Tootsie Roll captured me because it was so unique. My first thought was that I may never see that again, and my second thought was that God could give that to me if I would just pray for it. My goal was to give it away to a preacher when God gave it to me. The bible teaches in the book of Hebrews (A) 11:6 that without faith it is impossible to please him; for he that cometh to God must believe that he is, and that he is a rewarder of them that diligently seek him. I told my wife that I was going to pray for that Tootsie Roll and trust God to give it to me. We never mentioned it to anyone at the church or to any family member but God was moving behind the scenes on my behalf.

It was two days later when I was asked to go on the road with a man named Randy Lawson. We loaded up the truck and hit the road. As we were driving to the jobsite I told him about the huge Tootsie Roll I had seen and that I was trusting God to give it to me. He had seen the Lord do amazing things in the past for me, and I felt like he believed it would happen someday or someway. What happened next stunned both of us. While we were getting on I-275 to hit the freeway I pointed up above us and both of our eyes looked at a Tootsie Roll semi-truck driving the other way. I can honestly say in my thirty years of living that was the very first time I had ever seen a Tootsie Roll semi-truck.

Randy told me in twenty two years of driving and over forty four years of living that was his first encounter with a Tootsie Roll semi-truck, as well. The very next day we had to go to the same jobsite to work. As we were getting on I-275 again, at the exact same spot, it happened again. The Tootsie Roll semi-truck past by for the second straight day! As the Tootsie Roll semi-truck drove by again, Randy looked at me and said, "I can't believe that just happened."

The very next day was my birthday and the church had a surprise birthday party for me after services. We had cake and ice cream and I was very thankful for their kindness. After church was over, my in-laws invited me over to celebrate my birthday. I can still remember walking in the house and being approached by little Hunter. He had a present in his hand that he was eager to give me. I remember being extremely tired and totally exhausted. Hunter insisted that I open my gift before I did anything else. When I sat down and began opening my gift I discovered that God answered my prayer. My present was that Tootsie Roll that I had seen just a few days earlier. Thank God He is still on His throne and He really does care for His children.

HEBREWS 11:6: *But without faith it is impossible to please him: for he that cometh to God must believe that he is, and that he is a rewarder of them that diligently seek him.*

THIRTEEN

A SAD STORY THAT STILL BREAKS MY HEART

LUKE 16:23: *And in hell he lift up his eyes, being in torments, and seeth Abraham afar off, and Lazarus in his bosom.*

OFTEN TIMES, THROUGH LIFE, things are bound to come our way that saddens our day and sometimes even tests our faith. Life can be like a roller coaster at times and it is how we handle each trial and tribulation that will determine whether we grow or die as a Christian. Job (A) 1:21 says, "Naked came I out of my mother's womb, and naked shall I return thither: the LORD gave, and the LORD hath taken away; blessed be the name of the LORD." Life at times will be great, but at other times it feels like you can't take another step. Job was on top of the mountain one day and lost it all the next day. Sometimes the trial of your faith worketh patience and God is trying to build your strength in Him through sudden bad news that comes your way. I've learned through the years that God's word has every answer for every problem we will ever face in life. Never trust in your feelings but rather in God's unchanging promises.

Often in my life many pains, heartaches, tragedies, surprises, and sudden deaths have tried to derail me from the shining path. If it wasn't for God's word I would have more questions than answers. Thankfully I have always understood that God's hand can be seen in every triumph or tragedy that is sent my way. Although I could give you many different stories in my life that shocked me, one in particular stands out to me. This story breaks my heart and it is sobering to say the least. This is a true account that proves the severity of making fun of the word of God. Your heart will be enlarged with faith as you read this story from my past. To this day it troubles me and fills my soul with grief. Here is a story that will stick with you for years to come.

When I first started working at Poco, I was introduced to a man who was happy to test my faith in every way he could. He worked me harder and treated me worse than any other person at my job. Over the course of time, I began to earn his trust and prove to him that I was a true Christian. This man was a rough, tough and rugged individual who had a sinful past. We became pretty close to each other and he told me that I was the only person on earth he would talk to about God. Every once in a while he would ask me different questions about heaven and hell and I would do my best to answer him according to the bible. He became precious to me and I developed a heavy burden for his soul. This man struggled with heart problems and health was a chief concern for him. After a few episodes with his heart, and many days of missing work, he sadly lost his job. My heart went out to him and I wondered how I could help him.

Around three weeks after he was fired, the Spirit of God strongly urged me to visit his home and offer him some aid in any possible way I could. As I followed God's leadership and drove to his house, something terrible was about to happen.

To be honest, I expected a warm welcome by this man as I planned on giving him some money and a CD about hell. As I knocked on the door I was greeted by this man's wife who saw my bible and cursed me off the porch. Her words were extremely blasphemous and dangerous. She talked to me like an animal rather than a human and made it clear that I never come back. As I left her porch and made it back to my car, the Holy Spirit pleaded with me to stay as long as it took. Sitting in my car that day and thinking about what just took place made me very uneasy and very worried for that lady. After about seven minutes of waiting the man I went to see came outside and apologized on his wife's behalf and invited me in with open arms. He told me that his wife answered because he was sleeping and was sorry for how she treated me.

We talked that day for around thirty-five minutes and many kind words were exchanged. At the end of our conversation I asked him if he would listen to a CD on hell because I may never see him again. He promised me he would and thanked me for my visit. The CD was called *Four Times Man Cannot Die.* This CD was filled with examples of folks dying too soon and opening their eyes in the flames of hell.

This would indeed be the last time we spoke and the last time we seen each other again. Around a year later, while at work as I was walking through the shop, my boss called me into his office. He gave me the news that the man I visited only a year earlier had passed away. He was in his early fifties. The news stunned me and caused me to inquire how he died. My first thought was that he most likely had a heart attack and that was how he left this world. However, after further research, we found out that he killed himself by putting a gun in his mouth and blowing his head off.

After hearing this news it made me wonder if what that woman said to me that day on her porch caused her to lose her husband. The bible says in Revelations (B) 21:8 "But the fearful, and unbelieving, and the abominable, and murderers, and whoremongers, and sorcerers, and idolaters, and all liars, shall have their part in the lake which burneth with fire and brimstone: which is the second death." When people laugh at the word of God, and despise His Spirit, this will be the final state of man. According to Proverbs (C) 6:15 "Therefore shall his calamity come suddenly; suddenly shall he be broken without remedy." I still miss my friend and I'm sure this woman will miss her husband. Life is but a vapor that appeareth for a little while then vanisheth away. (James (D) 4:14) When you laugh and make light of the Spirit of God, your life will quickly take a turn for the worse. Don't force God to take drastic measures in your life by provoking Him to anger. Be careful what you say and who you say it to.

JOB 1:21: *And said, Naked came I out of my mother's womb, and naked shall I return thither: the LORD gave, and the LORD hath taken away; blessed be the name of the LORD.*

REVELATIONS 21:8: *But the fearful, and unbelieving, and the abominable, and murderers, and whoremongers, and sorcerers, and idolaters, and all liars, shall have their part in the lake which burneth with fire and brimstone: which is the second death.*

PROVERBS 6:15: *Therefore shall his calamity come suddenly; suddenly shall he be broken without remedy.*

JAMES 4:14: *Whereas ye know not what shall be on the morrow. For what is your life? It is even a vapour, that appeareth for a little time, and then vanisheth away.*

FOURTEEN
GOD'S FAITHFULNESS IN MY LIFE

PSALMS 56:4: *In God I will praise his word, in God I have put my trust; I will not fear what flesh can do unto me.*

IT IS NO SECRET, to those who know me, that the grand old hymns of the faith play a major role in my everyday life. One of my hobbies is to study each hymn's history, and the men and women who penned them down. Nearly every hymn that is found in your hymnal came from powerful Christians who were writing under the inspiration of the Holy Spirit. When you deeply study the people, who God used to pen these songs, you will find that their impact still reaches the world hundreds of years after their deaths.

One of my favorite songs ever written is a song entitled, "Great is Thy Faithfulness." It was penned by Mr. Thomas Chisholm. This song expresses the faithfulness of God in a way that is honest and true. This song has played a big part in my life and the lives of countless thousands through the years. Mr. Chisholm wanted to tell the world about the faithfulness of God in his own personal walk through this song. Many Christians, all across this country, could stand up and testify about the love, grace and faithfulness of God throughout the pages of their life. I Corinthians (A) 10:13, tells us that God is faithful. Revelations (B) 19:11 says that God is faithful and true. No man or woman that has ever walked with God has been able to describe just how faithful Jesus really is. He is just, Holy, Pure, Matchless, Glorious, and Lovely. Hundreds of verses describe His Faithfulness toward His saints and I aim to give you examples, in this chapter that will prove it even more. When you read these examples, I want it to dawn on you how good God really is to each and every one of us.

The bible tells us in Psalms (C) 40:5 "Many, O LORD my God, are thy wonderful works which thou hast done, and thy thoughts which are to us-ward; they cannot be reckoned up in order unto thee; if I would declare and speak of them, they are more than can be numbered." There have been many times, in my life, when I found that verse to be true and wonderful while serving Him. It is humbling to know that out of seven billion people that inhabit earth, God has the ability to think about us individually. Allow me to explain what I am talking about through a few amazing stories that have came to pass in my life.

A few years ago, on a Saturday morning, my wife went downstairs to cook breakfast and noticed that water was leaking through the ceiling. Upon further investigation we discovered that the floor was rotting out in the upstairs bathroom and needed to be fixed immediately. We got a bucket and placed it under the spot where the water was leaking and began trusting the Lord for the funds to repair it. My wife was worried, but I never was. As the problem got worse, and the situation became darker, I told my wife that God would meet our need shortly.

The bible teaches, in Malachi (D) 3:10-11 that if we give to His work, He in return will rebuke the devourer and provide all our needs. The next day God answered our prayer and sent two men to our house to fix our problem. They paid for all the parts, charging nothing for the labor and in less than twenty-four hours they had everything finished. This would have cost us over a thousand dollars and drained us financially. God proved to us that day He is faithful and we were extremely thankful for what He did for us.

The second example of God's faithfulness in my life happened around Christmas time a few years ago. My work hours were low that winter, and we were struggling to pay the bills. My wife asked me one day how we were going to pay for Christmas, and I couldn't give her an answer. I remember telling her that God is faithful and He would send the money somehow. As we went to church that following Wednesday an awesome man asked if he could speak to me in private. He told me that God put it on his heart to give my wife and me one hundred dollars for Christmas gifts. His gift overwhelmed me and blessed my heart in a special way. Two days later, at my company Christmas party, my boss gave me an extra bonus that I was not expecting. When I opened the envelope I saw a check for five hundred dollars for more Christmas gifts. The bible teaches that the goodness of God will lead us to repentance. We had a beautiful Christmas that year and God proved, once again, His watchcare over our lives.

The third example of His faithfulness in my life took place just a short while ago. John the Baptist said, in Luke (E) 3:11 that if we have two coats we should impart to him that hath none and God will bless you. God laid it on my heart to find two people that needed a coat and give them each one coat. Both coats were used but they were very nice. One coat was black leather with the American flag on the back and the other coat was tan leather. It was the coat that I wore everywhere I went. Both men loved the coats, but my decision of giving my coats away left me with none. A few months later, on a Sunday morning, a young man approached me and said he had a gift for me. We went to his car and he pulled out the gift. To my amazement it wasn't money, shoes, or a bible, but it was a coat. He told me that God told him to get me a coat and make sure it was a nice one. The coat was made in England and was worth more than the other two coats combined. Once again God showed up in a timely way and attended to my need. Over and over, through out my life, God has been faithful to me, even though I have failed Him.

The next example that I'm going to share with you comes from a Sunday night service. God spoke to my heart about helping the pastor. As the man of God was preaching to his flock, God directed me to give him my golf clubs after the service that night. The clubs came from my dad, at Christmas one year, and were very much used. They were special to me and it was hard to give them away. After church that night my father-in-law asked my wife if I needed some golf clubs for any reason. I was amazed how quickly God replaced my clubs with other ones. After looking at the clubs I picked a couple of them that I would use and left the rest for someone else who may have needed them. About seven months later, at work one day, I received a call from my wife that ministered to my heart. She told me that her uncle called her and said he had a new set of golf clubs for me if I needed them. Some of the clubs were still in their factory wrappings and they were in great shape. It truly is great how God uses people to meet our needs, and wants. I love the old Charles Gabriel song that says, "I stand amazed at the presence of Jesus the Nazarene and wonder how he could love me a sinner condemned unclean."

The last example that I pray will bless your heart is simple, yet profound concerning God's faithfulness. Not long ago, after teaching the teens on a Sunday morning, God performed a miracle that others saw with their own eyes. The Lord told me to help a few people, and if I did he would help me. I reached in my wallet and grabbed everything I had and gave it away. After I did this I looked at my wife, in front of four people, and said,"Someone will take us out today and you don't have to worry about cooking this afternoon." Immediately after this statement was made I walked towards the auditorium and through two sets of doors and was stopped by my Grandpa. He told me that after church he was going to take us out to eat at a restaurant called Baldos. My wife and the other four people were standing there when he told me the news, and I looked at my wife and said,"God sure is good; isn't He?"

Psalms (F) 57:10 tells us God's mercy is great unto the heavens, and thy truth unto the clouds. The Lord has been so good to my family and me over the years, and has proved time and time again that He is faithful and true in my life. The bible says it best in Psalms (G) 62:8 "Trust in him at all times; ye people, pour out your heart before him: God is a refuge for us. Selah."

I CORINTHIANS 10:13: *There hath no temptation taken you but such as is common to man: but God is faithful, who will not suffer you to be tempted above that ye are able; but will with the temptation also make a way to escape, that ye may be able to bear it.*

REVELATIONS 19:11: *And I saw heaven opened, and behold a white horse; and he that sat upon him was called Faithful and True, and in righteousness he doth judge and make war.*

MALACHI 3:10: *Bring ye all the tithes into the storehouse, that there may be meat in mine house, and prove me now herewith, saith the LORD of hosts, if I will not open you the windows of heaven, and pour you out a blessing, that there shall not be room enough to receive it.*

11: *And I will rebuke the devourer for your sakes, and he shall not destroy the fruits of your ground; neither shall your vine cast her fruit before the time in the field, saith the LORD of hosts. That if we give to His work, He in return will rebuke the devourer and provide all our needs.*

PSALMS 40:5: *Many, O LORD my God, are thy wonderful works which thou hast done, and thy thoughts which are to us-ward: they cannot be reckoned up in order unto thee: if I would declare and speak of them, they are more than can be numbered.*

LUKE 3:11: *He answereth and saith unto them, He that hath two coats, let him impart to him that hath none; and he that hath meat, let him do likewise.*

PSALMS 57:10: *For thy mercy is great unto the heavens, and thy truth unto the clouds.*

PSALMS 62:8: *Trust in him at all times; ye people, pour out your heart before him: God is a refuge for us. Selah.*

FIFTEEN
SPECIAL DELIVERY, SPECIAL DELIVERY

PSALMS 78:25: *Man did eat angel food;*
He sent them meat to the full

ONE OF MY ALL time favorite songs, as I was growing up, was a song entitled, "God Delivers Again." It is a song about how God, through a man named Moses, parted the Red Sea and brought the children of Israel through on dry ground. Every time God's people encountered impossible circumstances, God always showed up exactly at the right time, and delivered them out of every situation.

All throughout the bible there is a rich history of God sending His people a "Special Delivery," when they least expected it. Jesus loves to give good gifts unto His children, and He does it on a daily basis. The word of God tells us in James (A) 1:17 "Every good gift and every perfect gift cometh from above." God is always seeking opportunities to send a special delivery from His storehouse of love, but we hinder Him many times through our unbelief. According to Mark 6:6, the bible teaches that Jesus wanted to bless His people in a marvelous way, but He couldn't because of their unbelief. We tend to doubt God rather than believe Him and that is why Christians have very few blessings in their everyday life. Hebrews (B) 11:6 says, "That without faith it is impossible to please Him." God has never changed, and He is willing and able to send something special your way, but you first must believe that He can.

A story that has always touched and blessed my heart is found in I Kings chapter 17 with a man called Elijah. The bible teaches in James (C) 5:16 that Elijah was just as much human as you and I but Elijah exercised more faith than you and I do. One day this man of God told King Ahab that through his word God would not allow it to rain on earth for the space of three and a half years. God told Elijah to go to the brook Cherith, before Jordan, because He had a Special Delivery for him there. God not only allowed Elijah to drink of the brook, He also, commanded the ravens to bring him food every morning and every night. There will be times, in the child of God's life, when God commands His spiritual mail carrier to bring you a delivery that is first class and right on time. This Chapter will cover several examples, in my life, where God sent me a delivery that was unexpected, but overwhelming in my walk with Him. Let me share these examples that blessed my heart, and I hope they bless yours.

Many years ago, while sitting in the house of God, I remember having a burden on my heart that nobody else even knew about. It was not mentioned to anyone, not even my parents, my wife, or my pastor. God spoke to my heart that night about taking my burden to the Lord and leaving it there. The bible says in James (D) 1:6 "To ask the Lord in faith, nothing wavering and it will surely come to pass." My heart was broken over the prayer when I started, but when I finished the Spirit of God made it clear that the need would be met. As I rose to my feet, I was approached by a man, almost instantly, with a gift in his hand. He asked if he could speak to me and I

said, "Sure." He told me that as I was praying, something told
him to write me a check for $100 dollars. He then handed me
the check and said I pray it will be a blessing to you. Praise the
Lord, it was exactly what I needed and it still blesses my heart
to this day.

Another special delivery from God, that blesses my heart,
happened at work when I was twenty five years old. A man that
worked with me, from time to time, said he needed to speak to
me and that it was urgent. I remember meeting him in the park-
ing lot, by his car, and I still remember his look of excitement;
like it was yesterday. He told me he had a special gift that he
wanted me to have. He then reached in his car and pulled out
a beautiful CD holder and it was brand new. He then told me
to look inside to see what it was. I opened it up and discovered
that it was the entire Old and New Testament of the bible on
CD. It was so thoughtful and my heart melted within me when
he handed it to me. That delivery from God still remains one of
the greatest blessings that I have ever received.

Allow me to give you another delivery, from a preacher
one day, that shook me while I was hitting golf balls at my
parent's house. My mom came outside and handed me a letter
and told me that I needed to read it. The letter was from a man
of God that has given his all for the Lord, and he has always
taken the time to help me in my journey with God. He told
me, through this letter, that a special gift was being sent be
way of FEDEX and it would be at my house in about a week.
The news stunned me and encouraged my heart as I waited for
this delivery. Around two weeks later the gift arrived like he
promised and my wife and I opened it together. The gift was
extremely unique and very rare. My wife asked me what it was
and I proudly and humbly told her that the gift was a copy
of five signatures of some of the greatest Christians who have
ever lived. Alongside their names were their own personal

life verses that meant so much to them. The gift blessed me because it came at a time when I was a little down about life, and wondered if anyone cared about me. My friend, I'm glad to report that God cares for you, and longs to meet your every need when you serve Him with a pure heart.

Something else that comes to mind is a delivery that came to me while I was very tired, late on the road, one night. At the time I was working long hours and there was no time to take breaks at all. It was the dog days of summer and we were on the go all day. David said, in the book of Psalms (E) 37:25 that in all his life he had never seen the righteous forsaken, nor His seed begging bread. My God promises us, through His word, that no matter how dark our situation looks He will take care of it for us if we can only trust Him. To say that I was hungry was putting it lightly. I remember my stomach growling while we were working that night. At that very moment, I remember asking the Lord for a miracle like he supplied in Matthew chapter 14 when He fed the five thousand with just five loaves and two fishes. To my amazement, less than five minutes later He did just that. I remember a man from M-DOT pulled up with a box of White Castle's sliders that fed about twenty people, including me. It came at a time when I felt weak and dizzy, and the timing was impeccable. God gave me strength the rest of the night. I thank and praise the Lord for His special delivery and answering my prayer. Don't ever give up on God, for He owns the cattle on a thousand hills and the clouds are nothing more than the dust off His feet.

Let me end this chapter with one more phenomenal story that will build up your faith in God. This story is a reminder of His provision in our life, and His constant watch care over us. A young man in our church accepted the Lord as his Savior and began to grow in the Knowledge of His Lord very fast. My heart's desire was to help him grow in any way I could, so

I gave him something that was dear to me to help him grow. After I made the decision to help this young man I decided to call my mother and ask her opinion on this matter. She said if God spoke to you about it, then do it and he will bless you for it. I then thanked her and hung up the phone. Joy filled my heart after our conversation and my decision to help this young man was confirmed. Later that night, when church was over, as I was preparing to leave, the pastor's wife stopped me. She told me that there was a special delivery for me but it was a secret who it was from. She handed me a blank envelope and walked away. When we got to the car I opened up the envelope and there was $50 dollars inside. To this day I have no idea who gave it to me, but I thank God for it anyway. We serve a Holy God that takes special interest in every move we make, and every step we take. The last phrase in the song, God delivers again, reads as follows: Just when things look hopeless my God delivers again.

JAMES 1:17: *Every good gift and every perfect gift is from above, and cometh down from the Father of lights, with whom is no variableness, neither shadow of turning.*

HEBREWS 11:6: *But without faith it is impossible to please him: for he that cometh to God must believe that he is, and that he is a rewarder of them that diligently seek him.*

JAMES 5:16: *Confess your faults one to another, and pray one for another, that ye may be healed. The effectual fervent prayer of a righteous man availeth much.*

JAMES 1:6: *But let him ask in faith, nothing wavering. For he that wavereth is like a wave of the sea driven with the wind and tossed.*

PSALMS 37:25: *I have been young, and now am old; yet have I not seen the righteous forsaken, nor his seed begging bread.*

SIXTEEN
WALKING BY FAITH NOT BY SIGHT

PSALMS 119:18: *Open thou my eyes, that I may behold wondrous things out of thy law*

TO BE HONEST, THE concept of walking by faith and not by sight is easier said than done. When I look around this country I quickly discover that this idea is almost a thing of the past. The Fanny Crosby's and Ira Sankey's of the world do not exist anymore.

The great Fanny Crosby was blind six months after her birth. She refused to ever use that as an excuse because she felt as though she could see things spiritually that people could never see. She was forced to walk by faith everyday of her life. She went on to write around 9,000 songs that have touched millions of lives. She had most of the bible memorized and she was a giving machine. Fanny Crosby sold around 1,000,000 copies of her works with every penny going to the Lord. Mrs. Crosby's life puts us all to shame and she could not even see like you and me. Doing what she did took a lot of faith and a lot of trust. Our biggest problem, or struggle in life, is that we want to make it work, without trusting in the Lord. Sometimes we need to let go of our problems and let God take over.

While working one day, my wife called me at around 11:00 a.m. in the morning to notify me that we needed glasses. I told my wife to make an appointment. She then told me that we really didn't have the money. I then responded that sometimes, in life, God wants us to trust Him and so she made the appointment. When I arrived home later that afternoon I asked if we had received any mail. She said yes we did. I then asked, "Was there a check?" She said, "Yes there was." She then told me it was a check for three hundred eighty five dollars. We went to the appointment at America's Best and both of us bought new glasses, and some new contacts. Altogether the cost was three hundred sixty five dollars. After the appointment we went to dinner with the remaining twenty dollars.

There must be times, in our lives, when we rely on Him whether we understand it or not. It was about a month later, while I was on the Internet, a commercial came on for America's best when I was posting this story about the glasses. That commercial was a reminder of God's goodness.

We need more moments like this in our lives as we walk with God. These moments are when we can reflect on His blessings. Like the old hymn says, "Count your many blessings. Name them one by one. And it will surprise you what the Lord has done."

SEVENTEEN

GOD SENDING US A NAME FOR OUR FIRST CHILD

I SAMUEL 1:27: *For this child I prayed; and the Lord hath given me my petition which I asked of Him*

WHEN MY WIFE AND I found out that we were going to have our first child, many thoughts ran through our minds. Naturally, at first, it was a shock that we were going to be parents. We also had the fear of the unknown and different emotions that we had never experienced before. The next feeling we had was joy like the bible teaches in John (A) 16:21. We then felt a bond like we have never known between us. We also thought about our future in a fashion like never before. Needless to say we were doing more thinking than ever before.

The bible teaches us to trust in the Lord with all our heart and lean not upon our own understanding. In all thy ways acknowledge Him, and He shall direct thy paths. We had to learn more than ever whether we understood it or not, God was going to help us every step of the way. God has always been there for us and there is never any reason to doubt Him. Jesus said in Hebrews (B) 13:5 that I will never leave thee nor forsake thee.

I can still remember when we had the ultrasound and found out we were having a little girl. Excitement filled our hearts and wonder did as well. At that point our minds began to shift to two things. Number one was having a healthy baby. That was such a concern that we had because I know story after story of people that had unhealthy children and the heartbreak that it can cause. One story always sticks out to me and it involves a great songwriter.

A mother once had the sorrow of losing eighteen children to death, and the nineteenth was sick also. She raised him for Christ and as a result he wrote over four hundred hymns and the famous song, OH HAPPY DAY! Can you imagine what that mother and father felt like as one child died after another. To be honest, we had a fear about the health of our little one, and was simply trusting Jesus to give us a healthy child.

Secondly, our next concern was baby names. Every name has a meaning and we were aware of that. Naomi, in the bible, means beautiful, but Mara means bitter. There is a long study about names that will bless your heart, found throughout the pages of history if you study it out. As we prayed about the right name for our child, we must have gone through 700 to 800 names. We didn't have peace about any of them. After weeks of searching for the proper name, we came up with three possible choices. The first was Ella because we felt that was a unique name. Next was Melody, which is a good bible name. Last, but not least, was Hope which is found all throughout the word of God. We wanted to consider all these names before making a final decision. After much thought and prayer God seemed to give us peace about the name Hope. Once God spoke to my heart, my wife and I agreed together that this was the name God gave us for our child. This was around five months before Hope's birth and we never questioned it again.

When the time came that my wife was to be delivered, we arrived at the hospital under the doctor's request. I felt like it was a mistake because the doctor was trying to speed up the process rather than letting it happen on God's timetable. For two days they tried to induce labor on my wife by using medications and other things but to no avail. My wife was then at her lowest point as we were sent home without a baby to hold in our arms. I assured my wife that God has a purpose for everything that happens in our lives and once it comes to pass we will then understand it. We returned to the hospital for another couple days of labor and pain. Praise the Lord at 2:15 a.m. the next morning, we held a beautiful, healthy little girl in our arms. Hope was born on August 24th 2010.

As we were packing up to leave the hospital, God told me to open my bible and when I did it opened up to Romans (A) 8:24 and as I was reading that verse God gave me assurance that He gave us her name. When looking at that verse it said, "for we are saved by hope: but hope that is seen is not hope: for what a man seeth, why doth he yet hope for?" That verse alone has the word hope in it more times than any verse in the bible, and that's when Hope was born 8:24. God works in mysterious ways and I found out later that Hope is considered the greatest word in the English language.

JOHN 16:21: *A woman when she is in travail hath sorrow, because her hour is come: but as soon as she is delivered of the child, she remembereth no more the anguish, for joy that a man is born into the world.*

HEBREWS 13:5: *Let your conversation be without covetousness; and be content with such things as ye have: for he hath said, I will never leave thee, nor forsake thee.*

ROMANS 8:24: *For we are saved by* hope*: but* hope *that is seen is not* hope*: for what a man seeth, why doth he yet* hope *for?*

EIGHTEEN

THE POWER OF PRAYER
CAN CHANGE EVERYTHING

JAMES 5:16: *The effectual fervent prayer*
of a righteous man availeth much.

WHEN I BEGIN TO think about the difference prayer has made in my life, it humbles me to the lowest degree. From the start of my life, to the place I am today, someone has always been praying for me. My Mom and Dad have always prayed for my safety, my future, and my soul. There have been many times throughout the course of my life when other's prayed and have rescued me from certain danger. Sometimes I feel His presence in a stronger fashion more than at other times, and I must conclude that others are praying for me.

My mother told me that when I was a baby I had a rare step in my spine that would eventually sever my nerves in the spinal column. That was a major physical problem for my future. She told me how Van Born Baptist Church prayed for days that God would heal my back. The doctors determined that only fifty people in America had this rare disorder and forty eight of them were paralyzed. The odds were stacked against me but God is a God that can do the impossible. When people are determined to intercede for others, God hears them. My mom told me that over night my back was healed and the doctors had no answer how it happened

The bible is full of supernatural events that took place through the power of prayer. Remember Elijah prayed 63 words in I Kings 18:36-39 and the fire fell from heaven. Daniel prayed to the Lord and God sent an angel to stop the mouth of the lion. When a nation prays together, it will always stay together.

Mr. D. L. Moody and Ira Sankey, the great duo of some of the best revivals this world has ever seen, had a special request to the God of heaven. They made it a goal to pray for $20,000 dollars for Mr. Moody's College without anyone else knowing about it. They labored and toiled in prayer all that night. When the morning finally came, they found that every penny they were seeking was accounted for. When you open God's word and begin to read, that is God speaking to you. But when you fall on your knees and pray, that is you speaking to God. Please permit me to show you a few examples of just how powerful prayer can be if we will get plugged into its power.

There was a church in Alabama that desperately needed help from God concerning repairs on their building. They sought God's face through prayer and desired that He would meet their need of $30,000 dollars. We were on vacation, at the time, and we loved the pastor and his family very much. One day when were visiting folks in the neighborhood for visitation a miracle was sitting at the house of God, and we didn't even know it. When we arrived back at the church the pastor noticed an envelope on the front steps. I remember when he opened the envelope and discovered that it was a check for $30,000 dollars. God answered his prayer in a way that was special and unique.

My dad began to wonder how this happened, and who sent him the check. After much research my dad found out that a church in Michigan sold its building and was looking to help other churches for the cause of Christ. Somehow and someway God put it on that church's heart to send a portion of the money to Alabama to Pastor John Joiner and his congregation. Prayer can open doors of opportunity in our lives if we would just do it more often.

Another story that blesses my soul is the story of George Mueller. He ran an orphanage with around 180 needy children. Bro. Mueller ran out of food one day and his children were hungry. Many started to complain about the situation and question where the food would come from. Bro. Mueller saw this not as an obstacle but rather an opportunity for God to do something great. He went on with his normal routine of setting the table and making sure everything was ready for supper. When everything was in place he had the children bow their heads in prayer. As he prayed he thanked God for the food that was about to come. When his prayer was ended they heard a knock on the door. Bro. Mueller opened the door and found a man standing there with an answer to his prayer. The man told the story how he was heading to town with a wagon full of food when all of a sudden his ride broke down. All the food would spoil if it were not eaten within a day. He asked if Bro. Mueller needed it and he said yes I do and so do these children. He invited the man in for dinner and everyone was fed and they had food to spare. God is in the business of helping His children through prayer.

While working one day, a man that has always been a blessing to me was facing pain that was extremely intense. He was passing kidney stones and he said this was not something new. I could tell he was very uncomfortable and he needed help. He asked me to pray for him because the pain was almost unbearable. Three days later they disappeared and he has never had them appear again. Sometimes God likes to prove that He is still in control of all challenges that this world has to offer.

A preacher friend of mine had a tragedy strike his life that was sudden and heart breaking to put it kindly. His precious wife of over 40 years passed away with him holding her hand. They had a bond that was God given and she owned a good portion of his heart. Funds were tight for the man of God and the funeral was very costly. The preacher was at a loss for words and really didn't know how he would pay for the funeral. He began to pray earnestly about this need as his heart was broken. People began to give towards this need in a wonderful way. In just a matter of days a little over $17,000 dollars came in and it was just enough to cover all the costs. When I heard that story it blessed my heart and helped me to realize that anything is possible when prayer is involved.

Let me give you a personal story that will sum this all up for us. Around one year ago today something happened at my work that was beyond description. I was informed, immediately upon arrival, on a Monday morning that my friend Justin was in a horrible accident and they were unsure if he would make it. Upon hearing the news I was in shock! Justin has always been a help to me and the news filled my heart with sorrow. A few minutes later my boss asked me to get on the golf cart because he had more details about this horrible accident.

My boss told me that Justin was found in a ditch with life threatening injuries and his head was face down in a pool of blood. They rushed him to the hospital where he received emergency assistance. It seemed like a hopeless case and a tragic outcome. Justin was in a slight coma and in danger of dying or never being the same. My boss asked if I could say a quick prayer for Justin because he was in fatal condition. I can remember saying a very quick prayer for him and being at peace about the whole situation. Around twelve minutes later we got new reports that Justin sat up in his bed. He was texting friends and family that he was fine. Although he was sore and beat up, he was responding without the help of others. This news was amazing and I was praising the Lord for what He was doing. Everyone was speechless and filled with wonder with what they just witnessed.

Two short weeks later Justin came back to work and surprised us all. Within that day we had an unbelievable conversation that we will never forget. Justin's first question to me was, "Were you praying for me." Very quickly I said, "Yes." He said, "Thank you Tony, I really felt like you were. "I then told him that he was lucky to be alive. He then said, "I sure am." From this point in our conversation I switched gears and asked him if he believed in angels. Justin responded that he did now! My response to him was, "good because I feel like you will meet one in the near future, so be ready." The very next morning Justin told me a phenomenal story. Justin told me that when he went home, after our conversation, that he became very hungry and he craved pizza. He said he drove to the nearest pizza joint and he was approached by a stranger. This stranger walked directly up to Justin and said, "You really should be dead right now" and walked away without ever buying a pizza. Justin said it stunned him because he was covered that night and it would have been hard for anyone to know he was in a serious accident a few weeks prior to that.

Everyday I walk by him at work I see a walking miracle that proves prayer works. Without prayer where would we be!

NINETEEN
THE AWFUL MISTAKE OF MOCKING GOD'S MAN

PROVERBS 1:26: *I also will laugh at your calamity;*
I will mock when your fear cometh;

MANY YEARS AGO, IN the United States of America, the vast majority of sinners and saints alike had a reverence for a holy man of God. When preachers made public appearances in the market places and in the local businesses, people would often stop and show respect to the man of God. History books tell us that when the great Charles Finney would appear in the factories of his day, people would turn off the machines, get on their knees and beg for forgiveness at just the sight of him. Mr. Finney had such a powerful testimony that sinners would fall under conviction simply by his walking into their building. Ask yourself, when is the last time you have seen anyone, in this generation have respect for a man of God like that?

In the eyes of God, the greatest position a man can occupy in this world is that of a preacher. People today will laugh, disrespect, backtalk, murmur, curse, and blaspheme a preacher and never think twice about it. Sometimes I cringe when I hear the way people talk and act around a man of God. In 2 Peter

(A) 3:3 the scriptures say, "Knowing this first, that there shall come in the last days scoffers, walking after their own lusts." In 2 Timothy (B) 3:8 the bible tells us the following, "Now as Jannes and Jambres withstood Moses, so do these also resist the truth; men of corrupt minds, reprobate concerning the faith." The bible says that there will be those who resist the truth and have corrupt minds. Proverbs (C) 30:12 teaches that there is a generation that is pure in their own eyes and yet is not washed from their filthiness. People all over this country have no filter on their language, their conduct or their actions. They treat the bible like a comic book and God's men like Bozo the Clown. Many people, down through the years have suffered judgement, pain, torment and even death for disrespecting a man of God. Please be careful not to put your tongue on a man of God in any way, shape or form.

The ministers of the gospel of Jesus Christ are special in God's eyes and He will protect them at all costs. The worst decision that a man or woman, boy or girl, will ever make is to laugh, mock or mistreat a man of God. Everyone I have ever seen, at my work, who has laughed at me or the bible are either fired, judged, or dead. We need an old fashioned moving of the judgement of God to sweep across this country like in days of old. In Judges (D) 16:30, when the Philistines made fun of Samson, little did they know that it would be their last day of life before they opened their eyes in a Christless hell. In the book of Numbers (E) 16:32, when Korah, Dathan and all the crowd rebelled against Moses, little did they know that God would open up the earth and drop them into the pit alive. This chapter will give you a few examples of the vengeance and wrath of God against those who have mocked God's men over the years. These accounts are sobering and heart stopping in there description and will make the hairs on your neck standup. Please consider these examples and allow them to minister to your heart.

Several years ago a young couple decided to have fun at a man of God's expense. This decision proved to be foolish and costly a few months later. Dr. Don Green was conducting a tent revival years ago and he was in the prime of his ministry at the time. Dr. Green has read through the bible over 170 times and he prays for 5 hours a day. He has pastored Parker Memorial Baptist Church for around 60 years and he is without a doubt one of the best men of God in this country. One day, while the meeting was going on, the young couple, I alluded to, made fun of the way Dr. Green was raising money for the tent meeting that week in the privacy of their own home. The young couple was expecting a new healthy baby in a couple months and was planning a good future for their child. When it was finally time for the child to be delivered, they were devastated when they discovered that their child was missing multiple fingers on each hand. The bible says in Numbers (F) 32:23 "But if ye will not do so, behold, ye have sinned against the LORD: and be sure your sin will find you out." When you say things you ought not to say about a man of God expect a whirlwind of heartache to come your way.

Another story that comes to my mind involves an incident from the great Percy Ray. If you ever take the time to study this man of God's life you will quickly realize that he is one of the greatest men ever to live. The stories that surround his ministry are nothing short of amazing. Dr Percy Ray was very unusual, very holy and extremely unique. His walk with God was something to behold and everyone knew he was an old fashioned man of God. Although I could use many different examples that would blow your mind concerning the faith, one in particular fits this chapter perfectly. This story will open your eyes like very few stories you will ever read. Allow me to tell you this jaw dropping story that should keep us all in line with God.

One day, as Dr. Ray was shopping in a convenience store down south, a woman approached him with tears flowing down her cheeks. She tapped him on the shoulder and asked to speak to him immediately. Trembling and shaking, she told Dr. Ray that she had said something she shouldn't have and she wanted him to forgive her. Dr Ray looked at the woman and told her that God already told me what you said and God wants me to give you a message. He then told her that in nine days she would be dead and her husband would bury her in that blue dress that she loved so well. Nine days later that lady was laying in the funeral home; and her husband buried her in that blue dress that she loved so well. When you cross spiritual lines, with the Lord, and God signs your death warrant your as good as dead.

The last story in this chapter comes from my own life, around three years ago, when I was 28 years old. This is a sad story and it happened while I was eating dinner with my wife and my daughter after a Sunday morning service. Please listen as I tell you this real story that still hurts me to this day. One Saturday night God spoke to my heart about teaching to the teens about the dangers of mocking God. That night God's spirit was very strong in my house and after my lesson was complete fear gripped my heart over this subject. The next morning, when I arrived at church, I was all business and the atmosphere was pretty quiet in the little room where we teach the teens. God's spirit was real that day and the class went very good. We talked about many stories that proved the subject at hand and hearts were touched in that room.

After church that morning, as my wife and I were driving home, I remember being very tired and really hungry. The message that morning drained nearly all of my energy and I looked forward to eating a good meal and resting that afternoon. After arriving at our home and sitting down to eat lunch something shocking was about to take place. Shortly after praying over the meal my phone rang and it was someone I hadn't heard from in a while. When I answered the phone the voice on the other end was very vile and full of cursing. This man was calling from a Detroit Tigers game and I could tell he was drunk. He said some foolish things about God and about the bible that I sure didn't appreciate. To make it worse, my family was sitting there and I was grieved in my spirit. As I hung up the phone, after this shocking phone call, I looked at my wife and told her that this man was in serious trouble for what he just did. It turns out that I was right because that night this man's wife was rushed to the hospital and stayed there for two weeks. They lost a great deal of their finances and his life has been down hill ever since.

God's word, God's spirit, and God's man are never meant to be messed with and when they are God will always get the final say. Isaiah (G) 1:20 says "But if ye refuse and rebel, ye shall be devoured with the sword; for the mouth of the LORD hath spoken it." God promises that certain punishment is headed your way when you treat the things of God with a disrespectful attitude. God records every idle word that mankind speaks and records them in His eternal Book. If you live a life of sin and foolishness it will be shouted from the housetop one day.

Hopefully this chapter has shed a light on this subject like you have never seen before. Never be guilty of crossing a man of God all the days of your life and you will be much better off.

2 PETER 3:3: *Knowing this first, that there shall come in the last days scoffers, walking after their own lusts, tells us that in the last days there will be those who mock God and walk after their own lusts.*

2 TIMOTHY 3:8: *Now as Jannes and Jambres withstood Moses, so do these also resist the truth: men of corrupt minds, reprobate concerning the faith. Says that there will be those who resist the truth and have corrupt minds.*

PROVERBS 30:12: *There is a generation that are pure in their own eyes, and yet is not washed from their filthiness. Teaches that there is a generation that are pure in their own eyes and yet is not washed from their filthiness.*

JUDGES 16:30: *And Samson said, Let me die with the Philistines. And he bowed himself with all his might; and the house fell upon the lords, and upon all the people that were therein. So the dead which he slew at his death were more than they which he slew in his life.*

NUMBERS 16:32: *And the earth opened her mouth, and swallowed them up, and their houses, and all the men that appertained unto Korah, and all their goods.*

NUMBERS 16:33: *They, and all that appertained to them, went down alive into the pit, and the earth closed upon them: and they perished from among the congregation.*

34: *And all Israel that were round about them fled at the cry of them: for they said, Lest the earth swallow us up also.*

35: *And there came out a fire from the LORD, and consumed the two hundred and fifty men that offered incense.*

NUMBERS 32:23: *But if ye will not do so, behold, ye have sinned against the LORD: and be sure your sin will find you out.*

ISAIAH 1:20: *says "But if ye refuse and rebel, ye shall be devoured with the sword: for the mouth of the LORD hath spoken it.*

TWENTY

THE LORD HEALING LITTLE HOPE'S BODY

MATTHEW 17:7: *And Jesus came and touched them, and said, arise and be not afraid*

MY WIFE AND I experienced a night that we will not soon forget. We were awakened at around 1:00 a.m. in the morning to find that our little girl, Hope, was lying in a pool of vomit. My wife rushed her into the bathroom and did her best to clean Hope up but it didn't last long. Hope quickly threw up again and again. We then were forced to take her to the hospital at around 1:45 a.m., where we remained for the rest of the night. Hope's fever began to rise and she threw up about every fifteen minutes on average. The car was a mess, we were a mess and more importantly, Hope was a total mess.

While at the hospital Hope got worse and worse as we began to worry about dehydration. When things kept getting worse, and we felt we were at our wits end, God was about to perform a miracle for us.

I remember reading my bible and starting at Matthew chapter one, trusting God to answer our prayers. At around 3:00 a.m., I came to Matthew chapter 8, when Jesus began his many different miracles. Hope was in the middle of throwing up for the fifteenth time. Things looked dark, but God's light was about to shine through. While reading Matthew (A) 8:14-15 God sweetly spoke peace to my soul. I saw in these verses how God touched Peter's Mother-in-law's, and immediately the fever left her. God seemed to speak to my heart that He had just did the same thing for Hope. I looked over at my wife and stroked my daughter's hair and said, "We can go home if you want because Jesus just healed little Hope." Many people heard me say those words and my wife said we probably should stay because we are here already. I replied okay but she is healed.

I'm proud to report that Jesus indeed healed little Hope and it was instant. Hope never again threw up that night and the fever left her. What first was a dark circumstance turned into a great blessing. We will always remember that miracle and we're forever thankful for it.

Sometimes like with the life of Lazarus, God may not show up when we want Him to, but rather in a time that is altogether perfect. God is always RIGHT ON TIME.

MATTHEW 8:14: *And when Jesus was come into Peter's house, he saw his wife's mother laid, and sick of a fever. 15: And he touched her hand, and the fever left her: and she arose, and ministered unto them.*

TWENTY-ONE
IF THAT ISN'T LOVE

I JOHN 4:10: *Here is love, not that we loved God, but that He loved us and sent His Son to be the propitiation for our sins.*

SOMETIMES THERE ARE SONGS, with lyrics and phrases that are so good it causes you to sing them all day long. The bible teaches, in Ephesians (A) 5:19, that we should allow the Lord to speak to us through Psalms, hymns, and spiritual songs and make them a part of our daily routine. When your down in the dumps, remember a good old gospel song and a smile will return on your face.

In this chapter, I will give you the story of how God gave me the third verse of one of the best songs that has been penned in this generation. Every song has a unique story behind it and this will be no different. This story still makes me smile whenever I think about it. God sends blessings our way that encourage our hearts, and inspire us to tell others about His wonderful love. This story will stand out in your mind as a miracle, and will prove to you that God's love is real. If you are someone who has never experienced the love of Christ, then allow this simple story to convince you today.

A few years ago at my work, God overshadowed me in a way that was beautiful and transparent. The only thing that seemed to race through my mind that day was a song by Dottie Rambo entitled, "If That Isn't love." This song expresses the love of God, like few songs can, and has always spoken to this sinner's heart. Over and over again I can remember singing that song and God's spirit growing sweeter, the more I dwelt on the words.

As I stepped outside, I recall singing the chorus of that song which says, "If that isn't love the Ocean is dry, there's no stars in the skies, and the sparrow can't fly." What's amazing about this is that a sparrow flew right in front of me when I was singing that song. God spoke to my heart in a glorious way and showed me that His love was real, and He sent a sparrow to prove it to me. Less than five minutes after this incident took place, God gave me the words to the third verse of this grand old song.

The words read like this, "Jesus in power has risen, forgiving you and me, and one day by grace I shall see Him, through the blood that He shed for me."

The following Sunday I sang that song and God's Spirit moved in a powerful way and many lives were touched. A Godly song is like water to a thirsty soul, and we need to drink from the Lord's fountain every day. Colossians (B) 3:16 says, " let the word of Christ dwell in you richly in all wisdom; teaching and admonishing one another in Psalms and hymns and spiritual songs, singing with grace in your hearts to the Lord."

EPHESIANS 5:19: *Speaking to yourselves in psalms and hymns and spiritual songs, singing and making melody in your heart to the Lord;*

COLOSSIANS 3:16: *Let the word of Christ dwell in you richly in all wisdom; teaching and admonishing one another in psalms and hymns and spiritual songs, singing with grace in your hearts to the Lord.*

TWENTY-TWO
HOME SWEET HOME

LUKE 19:5: *And when Jesus came to the place, he looked up, and saw him, and said unto him, Zacchaeus, make haste, and come down; for to day I must abide at thy house.*

IF I HAD ONLY one message to give that would help this generation of teens, it would be a message found in Matthew (A) 6:33, "But seek ye first the kingdom of God, and his righteousness; and all these things shall be added unto you." Jesus has given us a promise in this verse that has never failed anybody in the past, nor will it ever fail anyone in the future. It was the single greatest verse that helped me through my teenage years and it saved me from many hard times and scars in my early years. The bible clearly tells us, in this verse, to seek the kingdom of God and His righteousness above any other thing that life has to offer. If you do this, God in return will give you anything that you need. You must make Jesus first and foremost in your life if you want a bright future to come your way.

Far too many people plan on one day having a big house, a car, a boat load of money, fun times, and a wonderful family on their own abilities without the Lord as their foundation.

This philosophy will lead to disappointment, sorrow, and many tears. Without the Lord, as the center of our life, we will have a future built on sinking sand and total disaster according to the word of God. People love to use God as the spare tire in their road of life, and only wish to reach out for Him after their lives are in a total ruin. This way of thinking is completely opposite of God's plan for our life and we wonder why things are not turning out right. The bible plainly states that Jesus must be our first option, for every need we have in life, if we want His blessings in return. Allow me to explain both sides of life the best way I know how.

First, there is a blessed side of life that we can enjoy if we rely on God for everything, rather than ourselves. The bible teaches in Psalms (B) 23:6 that surely goodness and mercy shall follow me all the days of my life; and I will dwell in the house of the LORD forever. Notice how goodness and mercy shall follow you, all the days of your life. God promises to bring things into your life when you put Him first.

Proverbs (C) 28:20, "A faithful man shall abound with blessings: but he that maketh haste to be rich shall not be innocent." Isaiah (D) 40:31, "But they that wait upon the LORD shall renew their strength; they shall mount up with wings as eagles; they shall run, and not be weary; and they shall walk, and not faint." Malachi (E) 3:10 teaches that on this blessed pathway God is able to open up the windows of heaven and pour out blessings every day.

When you journey through life in the blessed way; that doesn't mean you will never have problems, it just means you will never have problems by yourself. Proverbs (F) 18:24, "A man that hath friends must shew himself friendly: and there is a friend that sticketh closer than a brother." Hebrews (G) 13:5, "Let your conversation be without covetousness; and be content with such things as ye have: for he hath said, I will never leave thee, nor forsake thee."

When you walk with God on a daily basis, your path will be filled with light, joy, peace, safety, goodness, faith, love, meekness, treasures, shelter, grace, forgiveness, glory, assurance, and salvation. Simply put, your cup of blessings will be running over if you put Him first. In the blessed way, God will order your steps, and give you the desires of your heart. That is the right path that everyone should travel on, according to the scriptures.

Secondly however, I'm sad to say, there is another path that is available to you that the majority of mankind is finding themselves on. This path is a path of darkness, cursing, and self-righteousness that makes God unpleased. God is a jealous God, according to His word and He wants you to make Him first place in your life. Most teens, and adults alike, are on a broad path that is leading them to destruction, and they don't even realize it. The bible says in Proverbs (H) 14:12, 'There is a way which seemeth right unto a man, but the end thereof are the ways of death."

The bible teaches that when man leaves God's plan for their life and tries to put their own life together, they are headed for danger. The bible says in James (I) 4:17, "Therefore to him that knoweth to do good, and doeth it not, to him it is sin." The bible teaches us in 1 John (J) 2:15 to love not the world, neither the things that are in the world. If any man love the world, the love of the Father is not in him. In Psalms (K) 9:17, "The wicked shall be turned into hell, and all the nations that forget God."

When something else is first in your life, it has become an idol and you will soon forget God. Once you forget God, and make other things your goal in life, this is when Satan steps in where God is supposed to be. When this starts to take place, trouble begins to come your way and hard times will multiple for you. The bible teaches in Luke chapter 4 that Satan is the god of this world, and he will give you anything you desire as long as you forget about God. The Devil may seem like your friend, but the bible teaches he is a liar, a murderer, a roaring lion, and a master deceiver. He seeks to destroy your life through hurtful lusts, sin, and pleasures that will never last. On this path the bible teaches that it is slippery, dangerous, violent, punishing, and deadly. Proverbs (L) 3:33, "The curse of the LORD is in the house of the wicked: but he blesseth the habitation of the just." The bible teaches that everyone who travels this way is cursed.

Proverbs (M) 4:19, "The way of the wicked is as darkness: they know not at what they stumble." The bible tells us that the wicked constantly abide in darkness, and stumble through life. Proverbs (N) 13:15 declares that life is hard for those on this path. Proverbs (O) 13:21 says, "Evil pursueth sinners: but to the righteous good shall be repayed." The bible teaches that evil pursueth after sinners, or in other words, follows those on this path. People often wonder why life is so hard, but they never serve God and make Him the pinnacle of their lives. The longer you stay on this path of selfishness, and self-dependence, the farther you get from God's will for your life. Many people who stay on this path become vain, greedy, covetous, and far to busy building their own empire. The bible teaches in Luke (P) 12:21, "So is he that layeth up treasure for himself, and is not rich toward God." It also states, in Mark (Q) 8:36, "For what shall it profit a man, if he shall gain the whole world, and lose his own soul?" Always remember that anything you hold in your hand down here you will surely leave to others.

When God is removed from your mind, you will make very foolish decisions and destroy your life forever. Psalms (R) 14:1 says the fool hath said in his heart there is no God. Fools make a mock at sin and take the things of God lightly. Romans (S) 6:23 says the wages of sin is death and the soul that sinneth shall die. When the Lord is not important in your life your chances of success disappears. Please be sure you avoid this path, at all costs! Follow the Lord with all your heart. I would venture to say that in my entire life I have only seen a handful of young people choose THE BLESSED PATH for their life. Sadly, in contrast, I have witnessed hundreds of people pick the cursed path and it has devastated their future with God.

For every Joseph, David, and Daniel, found in the will of God there are millions found in the will of the Devil. It is sad to see such a small percentage do what Jesus said in Matthew (A) 6:33. We, as teachers and preachers, can only point people in the right direction, but we do not have the ability to live their lives for them. My goal and wish, through this chapter, is to cause someone to develop a hunger for God that has never been there before. My life has been a prime example of someone who has always tried to put God first, and could care less about achieving my own personal dreams. Never, in my childhood growing up or even in my teenage years, did I ever attend a party to fit in with others. Praise the Lord, I have never smoked a cigarette or touched alcohol in my life. I've tried to live clean and holy and if I would slip, in any way, I would repent very quickly.

Though my teenage years were rough at times, I never dropped out of church, and strived to stay faithful to the Savior. God has been so good to me, and has rewarded me for putting Him first. Although I never worried about a car, over time He gave me a Ford Mustang show car. Even though I didn't date a girl until I was twenty-five years old, God allowed me to meet my wife at church. Never did I even think about having a child, and God gave me a beautiful little girl later down the road. God has also given me a job that I love and too many blessings to number. The progress and advancement of my life is not due to planning but do to the Lord fulfilling His promise in Matthew (A) 6:33. God cannot lie. Titus (T) 1:2, "In hope of eternal life, which God, that cannot lie, promised before the world began; and my life is living proof of that."

Last year, nearly every day of the year, God used people to bless my family. With the remainder of this chapter please allow me to give you two stories that help prove that God will take care of you if you serve Him with ALL YOUR HEART.

The first story I want to give you is from one of the greatest Christians ever to breathe God's air. His name was Isaac Watts and his story is proof of God's provision in one's life. The second story will be how God worked things out to bless us with the home we enjoy now. I pray these two stories will speak to your heart and show you the importance of putting the Lord above anything and everything this world has to offer. Let me first start with Mr. Isaac Watts and show you the grace of God in his journey with Christ.

Isaac Watts was, without a doubt, one of the smartest, most gifted and spirit filled Christians that this world has ever seen. He is referred to as the Father of hymnology. Mr. Watts introduced his own personal hymns to his church, and the church embraced and supported them in a wonderful way. Mr. Watts went against the traditional thinking of how songs were sung in churches all across the world. Before Isaac Watts came along, only the Psalms were sung in church services and anything else was considered blasphemy.

Mr. Watts wrote biblical, uplifting and Christ honoring songs that became rapidly very popular and spread to other congregations across the world. Many different revivals, throughout the pages of time, can largely be attributed to the hymns that Mr. Watts wrote. He had already mastered four languages before the age of thirteen, and wrote many of his six hundred plus songs before the age of twenty. Mr. Watts wrote what many consider the greatest song in English history entitled, "When I survey the wondrous cross." Isaac Watts also wrote one of the greatest Christmas songs ever penned as well entitled, "Joy to the world." The bible teaches in 1 Corinthians (U) 3:6," I have planted, Apollos watered; but God gave the increase."

Music prepares the heart for preaching; and preaching helps draw people to Christ for salvation. Godly music and powerful preaching work together to speak to the lost and both, in their own way, can awaken a dead soul for Christ. Every soul that walks the aisle, through an Isaac Watts song, is fruit that is added to his account. It is widely known that Isaac Watts wrote a song entitled, "At the Cross." This song was one of the key factors in the great Fanny Crosby coming to Jesus in faith and repentance.

Mrs. Crosby wrote over nine thousand songs and walked with the Lord as close as any woman in the last thousand years. She won thousands upon thousands to the Lord through her own hymns and impacted this world like very few ever have. Every life touched and every soul reached for the Lord through her music can be traced back to Mr. Isaac Watts. The bible teaches he gets credit for his influence of planting the seed in the case of Fanny Crosby.

Mr. Isaac Watts also wrote the song entitled, "Am I a soldier of the cross." This one song was the key component in starting one of the greatest teams in gospel history which was D.L.Moody and Ira Sankey. Through this song, and its impact on their partnership, it kick started some of the best revivals this world has ever known. Multitudes were saved from the fires of hell through these revivals and Mr. Isaac Watts was an influence on every one of them.

Mr. Watts also wrote a song that made a major difference in the life of an Olympic hero by the name of Eric Lindell. Brother Lindell won Olympic medals for his country and heavenly treasures for his Savior. Through one of the old hymns that Isaac Watts wrote, many years before Eric Lindell felt God tug at his heart, and it caused him to give the rest of his years as a missionary to China. The story is told that when he boarded the ship to sail to a foreign land, thousands gathered to bid him farewell that day. With tears in his eyes, he led the people in the Isaac Watts hymn that affected his own life so deeply. For nineteen years Lindell served in China, in submission to God, and Isaac Watts was a big reason why.

His songs have stood the test of time and it is safe to say that his legacy is beyond compare. He wrote many books including a children's book that sold 80,000 copies in the first year and is still selling today. Many other stories surround this man's life, but I want to give you a story that relates to this chapter.

Isaac Watts was a frail man in stature, but a giant in faith. He worked night and day to advance the kingdom of God, and he was rewarded in a very unique way. People say he was short, unattractive and physically very weak. A woman fell in love with him one day through his beautiful poetry and longed for a chance to meet him in person. The story is told that her wish was granted one day and she was extremely disappointed. She was completely turned off by his appearance and broke his heart by running away. Mr. Watts took this experience as a sign from God never to marry anyone, but rather give his life as a servant for His Master.

Between pastoring, writing books, producing hymns, and serving others his body gave out on him at only twenty-eight years old. Isaac Watts became a little worried about his future, and wanted to resign his role as the shepherd of his flock. When he addressed his people about his health, a wealthy family in his church refused the notion of him resigning, and offered that he stay at their home, until he figured things out. Isaac quickly agreed to their generous offer and continued his work for God. Isaac was only suppose to stay at this couples home for two weeks but he ended up staying for the next thirty-eight years.

God blessed Mr. Watts dedication and paid for every meal, sheltered him with a home he never paid for and let him live in comfort for the majority of his life. Isaac Watts' life proves that God is a debtor to no man and the fountain of blessings will flow in our lives if we will make Him the heart-beat of our future. Isaac Watts may have been unattractive to this world, but he is glorious in the world to come.

For the rest of this chapter I would like to share with you a similar story of how the precious Lord blessed us with our home in a special way. The Lord deserves all the credit in this story and I lift up holy hands in praise for what He has done.

When my wife and I were engaged to be married, the search for a home quickly became a top priority in our lives. We began to look at many houses, apartments, and other places and every situation seemed to offer hope but always fell through the cracks of possibility. Before we knew it, the time had come to be married and we were still unsure of where we were going to live.

After our honeymoon was over, we still had no place to live, and we were trusting God in a fashion we never had before. My parents offered us a place to sleep in their garage, for a few days, while we continued to look for a home. My uncle also allowed us to stay in his house while they went on vacation for a week and it seemed like the door of opportunity was closing for us. After a few more days of searching, we then looked at some apartments in Belleville, Michigan. We thought that any place is better than no place. After meeting with the manager in charge we signed a one-year agreement to live there. The apartment cost $625.00 a month and it was like putting our money in a bag with holes in it; like the word of God teaches. We were told to make a one hundred dollar deposit towards the apartment, but they gave us two weeks to get out of our lease if something better came along. The very next day God had wonderful news for us that would change everything.

My uncle told me that a Christian man from his church had a condo for sale in Canton, Michigan and that we really needed to look at it. When my uncle said that to me something in my soul told me to take his advice. The next day my wife and I traveled towards Canton to look at the condo. After meeting with the owners, and walking through their home, God gave me peace that this was the right place for us. God worked it out for us and blessed us through out the entire process of finding a home we could call our own.

The condo originally cost $89,000 dollars a few years prior, and we ended up paying $42,000 dollars for it. We also had a wonderful, godly real estate lady by the name of Pam Hicks, who helped us with the condo. She helped us every step of the way. She was great throughout the whole experience and was a blessing to my wife and me. Pam Hicks paid around $850 dollars that we didn't have, to help us get our condo. All in all, we saved around $50,000 dollars on our condo and God's handprints could be clearly seen. God placed us in a wonderful community, with awesome neighbors, and gave us a beautiful starter home. There is no way to explain why God was so gracious to us, but all I can say is faithfulness really pays off. Put God first and you will begin to see your life come together in a perfect way.

MATTHEW 6:33: *But seek ye first the kingdom of God, and his righteousness; and all these things shall be added unto you.*

PSALMS 23:6: *Surely goodness and mercy shall follow me all the days of my life: and I will dwell in the house of the LORD forever.*

PROVERBS 28:20: *A faithful man shall abound with blessings: but he that maketh haste to be rich shall not be innocent.*

ISAIAH 40:31: *But they that wait upon the LORD shall renew their strength; they shall mount up with wings as eagles; they shall run, and not be weary; and they shall walk, and not faint.*

MALACHI 3:10: *Bring ye all the tithes into the storehouse, that there may be meat in mine house, and prove me now herewith, saith the LORD of hosts, if I will not open you the windows of heaven, and pour you out a blessing, that there shall not be room enough to receive it.*

PROVERBS 18:24: *A man that hath friends must shew himself friendly: and there is a friend that sticketh closer than a brother.*

HEBREWS 13:5: *Let your conversation be without covetousness; and be content with such things as ye have: for he hath said, I will never leave thee, nor forsake thee.*

PROVERBS 14:12: *There is a way which seemeth right unto a man, but the end thereof are the ways of death.*

JAMES 4:17: *Therefore to him that knoweth to do good, and doeth it not, to him it is sin.*

1 JOHN 2:15: *Love not the world, neither the things that are in the world. If any man love the world, the love of the Father is not in him.*

PSALMS 9:17: *The wicked shall be turned into hell, and all the nations that forget God.*

PROVERBS 3:33: *The curse of the LORD is in the house of the wicked: but he blesseth the habitation of the just.*

PROVERBS 4:19: *The way of the wicked is as darkness: they know not at what they stumble.*

PROVERBS 13:15: *Good understanding giveth favour: but the way of transgressors is hard. Declares that life is hard for those on this path.*

PROVERBS 13:21: *Evil pursueth sinners: but to the righteous good shall be repayed.*

LUKE 12:21: *So is he that layeth up treasure for himself, and is not rich toward God.*

MARK 8:36: *For what shall it profit a man, if he shall gain the whole world, and lose his own soul?*

PSALMS 14:1: *The fool hath said in his heart, There is no God. They are corrupt, they have done abominable works, there is none that doeth good.*

ROMANS 6:23: *For the wages of sin is death; but the gift of God is eternal life through Jesus Christ our Lord.*

TITUS 1:2: *In hope of eternal life, which God, that cannot lie, promised before the world began.*

1 CORINTHIANS 3:6: *I have planted, Apollos watered; but God gave the increase.*

TWENTY-THREE

GREAT SERVICES THAT I HAVE BEEN IN OVER THE YEARS

ISAIAH 64:1: *Oh that thou wouldest rend the heavens, that thou wouldest come down, that the mountains might flow down at thy presence,*

I HAVE TRIED MY best, over the years, to study some of the greatest revivals that have ever been recorded through the pages of time. Great men, through a greater God, have been instrumental in making a tremendous difference for Jesus. The apostle Peter preached on the day of Pentecost and 3,000 were born again. Jonah preached a message of repentance and all of Ninevah believed God from the greatest to the least of them. Spirit filled men of God like Charles and John Wesley saw thousands upon thousands converted to the Lord and totally transformed through a salvation experience. They said when Jonathan Edwards preached, during the great awakening, revival spread to multiple parts of the world and people were afraid of waking up in hell before the morning hit.

Many stirring messages have been thundered throughout the ages with results that have stood the test of time. When God's presence can be felt in a service, lives will be touched, souls will be converted, and a real difference will be made. Great services are almost a thing of the past and Christians all around this country long for the days of old when God seemed to move among his people. The purpose beyond this chapter is to prove that God is still in control, and that He is still in the soul saving business.

In this chapter I will share with you some of the very best services that I have ever been apart of. Lord willing, this will help you to realize that even though we are in the last days, God is still interested in changing lives and blessing His children. You will read a handful of powerful services that the good Lord has allowed me to be a part of through the years in this chapter. May God bless your heart as you read these stories.

Many years ago, at Open Door Baptist Church in Detroit, Michigan, God gave us an amazing service one day. I remember waking up on a Sunday and playing a gospel music tape while I was getting ready for church. God seemed to burn a particular song I was listening to in my heart and mind. The song was entitled, "Drifting to far from the shore" and that morning I listened to that song around fifteen times as I prepared myself for church. Peace came over my soul and I was absolutely positive God wanted me to sing that song, at church, that morning. Sure enough that Sunday morning, the pastor asked me to sing a song that was on my heart.

Before I sang my song, I gave a testimony of how God dealt with me about the song I was going to sing and I believe somebody needs to get right with God today. After my song was over I sat down to hear what the pastor was going to say. He stood up and said a statement that I will never forget. He told the congregation that he had a message that he studied for all week, that he really wanted to preach, but God would not allow him. Instead he told us how the Lord changed his message, in the middle of the night, to a message entitled,

"Drifting to far from the shore." My song fit his message like a glove and the power of God filled the air. When the invitation was given that morning the altar was covered with people pouring their hearts out to God. A number of people were saved and many more were helped. It was a service from heaven and it's impact is still being felt to this day.

Another service that comes to mind is a service that took place in Lansing, Michigan a few years ago. This service was special to me, and to all that attended that night. Even before the service began, in the car ride there, we could sense something glorious would happen in the meeting that night. As we were going down the road, a song came on entitled, "He didn't through the clay away." For some reason, the words in this song jumped out that day like never before. A man I was riding with never heard the song before, and kept playing it over and over again as he wiped tears from his eyes. The song speaks of God" ability to forgive those who have made mistakes in their past. Only God has the power to forgive and forget mistakes we have made over the years. We can forgive, but we do not have the ability to forget things in our past. This song is very special and it sure did touch our hearts on our way to the house of God that night.

When we arrived in Lansing to hear the word of God, something amazing happened just prior to the preaching. A man stood up, who had been converted a couple of years before, and sang the same exact song we heard on the way to church that night. When he was singing that song, people shouted, cried, rejoiced, and glorified God. The pastor of that church announced to his people that this song did more for his spirit than any other song he had ever heard. The pastor asked him to sing it over and over again and the Spirit of God completely took over. As he sang, people ran to the altar, gave away money, and revival swept through the church.

After the song service was concluded, and it was time for preaching, the service was about to reach new heights as the man of God started his message. The man of God preached from Jeremiah (A) 18:1 about the potter and the clay. He preached with total liberty that night and many lives were helped. The whole service flowed together in perfect harmony and they had a wonderful meeting that week. When God is in a meeting, it will always have the potential of being great. Let me give you two more services that I consider great over my years of walking with the Lord.

One night, at Midwestern Baptist College, I witnessed a scene that I will always remember. A friend of mine, who was actually the best man in my wedding, preached a life-changing message to those in attendance that evening. As he was delivering his sermon, to a crowd of around 700 that night, the power of God fell on him in a manner I had never seen before. In the white heat of preaching, under the influence of the Holy Ghost, this man jumped on the pulpit and was preaching from on top of the pulpit. This man is short in stature, but powerful in faith. Everyone in attendance wondered how he did that, and I must admit I did too. The service was indescribable and it spoke to many hearts. The bible teaches in Romans (B) 8:31, "What shall we then say to these things? If God be for us, who can be against us?" As I look back on that experience I believe God was with us that night and it felt like the gates of hell could not prevail against us.

The final great service I wish to bring to your attention was at Open Door Baptist Church's tent meeting in Detroit, Michigan. To this day it still remains one of the greatest services I have ever been a part of in my thirty one years on earth. The Spirit of God seemed to hover over the tent that night as the preacher opened the bible. In the crowd were amazing servants of God, and also sinners that needed to hear from heaven. The preacher had unusual power resting on him that night as he started his message. I had never seen a group of people listen so well, and it felt like God's spirit was everywhere. His subject was,"How to have the power of God, on your life, and what it takes to get it."

There was a stillness to that service that was priceless and every soul looked to be touched. People filled the altar when he was finished and many gave their lives for the service of God. That one message helped me more than any other message that I have ever heard. It took me to a level with Christ that I had never known. Matthew (C) 5:6, "Blessed are they which do hunger and thirst after righteousness: for they shall be filled." The bible says that those who are hungry and thirsty for His righteousness shall be filled. As I got up from the altar, that night, I had a new desire to hunger after the Lord like never before.

In closing out this chapter, I will be the first to say that services around this country are just a shadow of what they once were, but they still do exist. The bible does teach that in the last days there will be a great falling away (2 Thessalonians (D) 2:3) and true men of God would be hard to find. After traveling to many churches around this country I must confess that what the bible teaches concerning the end time is indeed true. I've asked myself, on many occasions, where is the Lord God of Elijah. I wondered, in my heart, if the church of the living God still remains in these last dark days. I'm glad to report that I have witnessed His wonders in churches over the years and have felt His power on several occasions. Although the majority of churches have turned from the truth, some still stand with the Lord. Our job, as Christians, is to support these ministries and help in any way possible as God directs us. When you sense revival, in a church, do whatever it takes to keep the fire going. We are the biggest problem why God is not moving in our churches anymore and there is no one to blame but ourselves. D.L. Moody once said that Christians are like the Dead Sea, they take in everything they can but they give nothing away. Christians are like spiritual sponges that take from the church and add nothing to it. Allow revival to begin in your own heart and it will surprise you how big of a difference you can make. God can still move like in days gone by if we will only allow Him to.

JEREMIAH 18:1: *Thus saith the LORD, Go and get a potter's earthen bottle, and take of the ancients of the people, and of the ancients of the priests.*

2: *And go forth unto the valley of the son of Hinnom, which is by the entry of the east gate, and proclaim there the words that I shall tell thee.*

3: *And say, Hear ye the word of the LORD, O kings of Judah, and inhabitants of Jerusalem; Thus saith the LORD of hosts, the God of Israel; Behold, I will bring evil upon this place, the which whosoever heareth, his ears shall tingle.*

4: *Because they have forsaken me, and have estranged this place, and have burned incense in it unto other gods, whom neither they nor their fathers have known, nor the kings of Judah, and have filled this place with the blood of innocents.*

JEREMIAH 18:5: *They have built also the high places of Baal, to burn their sons with fire for burnt offerings unto Baal, which I commanded not, nor spake it, neither came it into my mind.*

6: *Therefore, behold, the days come, saith the LORD, that this place shall no more be called Tophet, nor The valley of the son of Hinnom, but The valley of slaughter.*

ROMANS 8:31: *What shall we then say to these things? If God be for us, who can be against us?*

MATTHEW 5:6: *Blessed are they which do hunger and thirst after righteousness: for they shall be filled. says that those who are hungry and thirsty for His righteousness shall be filled.*

2 THESSALONIANS 2:3: *Let no man deceive you by any means: for that day shall not come, except there come a falling away first, and that man of sin be revealed, the son of perdition.*

TWENTY-FOUR

CROSSING THE LINE
WITH GOD

PROVERBS 8:36: *But he that sinneth against me wrongeth his own soul: all they that hate me love death.*

WHEN YOU STUDY THROUGH the 66 books of the King James 1611 AD Bible, you will find many times where people crossed lines with God that proved to be deadly. We all understand the love and long suffering of a thrice Holy God through what Christ did on the cross. The sacrificial death on the cross still remains the greatest display of mercy and grace that has ever been known. The love of God is undeniable and it is the driving force of our faith, as we know it. The born again redeemed are trusting in nothing else than the death, burial and resurrection as our way to heaven. On the other hand, there is another side of God that is rarely expressed but is just as true.

The bible gives us hundreds of verses about judgement, damnation and death. I could personally take my bible and show you example after example of where God's patience ran out and people crossed an eternal line with God that suddenly ended their life. From Nabal disrespecting David, and God killing him, to Korah and his crowd going against Moses in Numbers (A) 16:32-34; God will always get the final say in these matters. The word of God says in Proverbs (B) 1:7, "The fear of the LORD is the beginning of knowledge: but fools despise wisdom and instruction." Basically, that verse is teaching us that you can never get past first base with God unless you learn how to fear Him.

The book of James (C) 3:8 says, "But the tongue can no man tame; it is an unruly evil, full of deadly poison." Jesus said in Matthew (D) 12:36, "But I say unto you, that every idle word that men shall speak, they shall give account thereof in the Day of Judgment." In verse 37, "For by thy words thou shalt be justified, and by thy words thou shalt be condemned" and in Luke (E) 12:5, "But I will forewarn you whom ye shall fear: Fear him, which after he hath killed hath power to cast into hell; yea, I say unto you, Fear him." In Proverbs (F) 29:1 we see He that being often reproved (or warned) hardeneth his neck, shall suddenly be destroyed, and that without remedy. In other words, God takes His Word very seriously whether we do or not. My Dad always taught me how to fear and respect God in my everyday life. His "life verse" is found in Hebrews (G) 10:31, "It is a fearful thing to fall into the hands of the living God." It is a powerful verse of scripture that stuck with me through my life growing up. This verse will be important with the story I am about to tell. After this story is finished I pray that you will have a new found respect for God.

One night, as we were visiting people in Detroit inviting folks out to church, something serious happened that is troubling to say the least. My Father and I were on Gilbert St. trying to witness for our Blessed Savior. We didn't know it, but to our surprise gang members lived in the majority of those houses on that street. That really didn't matter to either one of us because we had a heavy burden to reach the lost. As we began to knock doors on this street, we said a quick prayer for safety before we got started. I remember the third house we came to God opened the door for a great witness that I will never forget. Two young women, who obviously had problems, were listening very intently as the Gospel was going forth. My Dad was doing all the talking and I was doing all the praying.

As the witness was advancing and hearts were being touched, something tragic was about to happen that would change everything. I remember seeing a man, from a gang's house across the street, and he was approaching us at a rapid pace. Before we knew it he had engaged in our conversation in an abrupt way. He interrupted my Dad and began to mock the bible and the Lord Jesus Christ. He cursed God with the foulest language I've ever heard. My Dad tried to calm him down the best he could, but nothing seemed to work. Finally, in the heat of the moment, my Dad said to him this statement. "If God is not real, go get a gun and blow your head off and we will see if He is real." The man, in anger, retaliated by saying, "I'll get a gun and blow your head off." As the man left to get his gun, my Dad continued on like nothing ever happened. The two young ladies were in shock and assured us that he was crazy. My Dad then responded that he was not afraid of that man, but he would leave if they were uncomfortable. However, before he left he quoted the famous verse in Galatians (H) 6:7, "Be not deceived; God is not mocked: for whatsoever a man soweth, that shall he also reap." When my Dad said that verse something turned on in my soul and I knew that man was in serious trouble for what he had done.

Two days later, after church was over while we were dropping someone off, something caught my eye. On the telephone pole was a picture of a man that looked all too familiar to my Dad and I. As we looked closer we discovered that a man had died a day earlier and it happened to be the man that interrupted us. The police also were at that gang house. A number of the gang members, with their hands handcuffed behind their backs, were being arrested. The bible tells us in Psalms (I) 7:11 God judgeth the righteous, and God is angry with the wicked every day. Please be careful what you say, and when you say it because God's ears are open at all times.

NUMBERS 16:2: *And the earth opened her mouth, and swallowed them up, and their houses, and all the men that appertained unto Korah, and all their goods.*

33: *They, and all that appertained to them, went down alive into the pit, and the earth closed upon them: and they perished from among the congregation.*

34: *And all Israel that were round about them fled at the cry of them: for they said, Lest the earth swallow us up also.*

PROVERBS 1:7: *The fear of the LORD is the beginning of knowledge: but fools despise wisdom and instruction.*

JAMES 3:8: *But the tongue can no man tame; it is an unruly evil, full of deadly poison.*

MATTHEW 12:36: *But I say unto you, That every idle word that men shall speak, they shall give account thereof in the Day of Judgment.*

37: *For by thy words thou shalt be justified, and by thy words thou shalt be condemned.*

LUKE 12:5: *But I will forewarn you whom ye shall fear: Fear him, which after he hath killed hath power to cast into hell; yea, I say unto you, Fear him.*

PROVERBS 29:1: *He, that being often reproved hardeneth his neck, shall suddenly be destroyed, and that without remedy.*

HEBREWS 10:31: *It is a fearful thing to fall into the hands of the living God.*

GALATIANS 6:7: *Be not deceived; God is not mocked: for whatsoever a man soweth, that shall he also reap.*

PSALMS 7:11: *God judgeth the righteous, and God is angry with the wicked every day.*

TWENTY-FIVE

GOD BLESSING ME WITH McMANNA ON A HOT SUMMER DAY

PSALMS 34:8:0: *taste and see that the LORD is good: blessed is the man that trusteth in him.*

OFTEN, THROUGHOUT THE COURSE of life, many people lack in thanking God for his blessings; no matter how small they seem to be. Paul said in I Thessalonians (A) 5:18, "In every thing give thanks: for this is the will of God in Christ Jesus concerning you." It is the will of God for us to be thankful for everything we receive. The next time you read through your bible I challenge you to take notice of just how many times people are unthankful for God's grace in their lives.

One example, of people being unthankful in the bible, is when Jesus healed the ten lepers in Luke (B) 17:12-19, only one of them even said thank you. Paul said in the last days, that people would become unthankful. 2 Timothy (C) 3:2 says. "For men shall be lovers of their own selves, covetous, boasters, proud, blasphemers, disobedient to parents, unthankful, unholy," Matthew (D) 24:12 says, "And because iniquity shall abound, the love of many shall wax cold." I can still remember, very vividly, when God laid it on my heart to give a man

$1,000 dollars for Christmas one year. After I worked hard for the money and gave him the check, this man barely said thank you, and went on his merry way. I determined, from that moment on , never to take things I receive from others lightly and act like that man did with the blessings that may come my way. Whether it is a suit coat or a candy bar, I want to be sure they know I appreciate them thinking about me. Every blessing I receive, from the hands of others, I either write it down on a piece of paper or store it in my memory banks because I never want to forget it. Sometimes God puts it on people's hearts to be a blessing to me, and sometimes He takes it upon Himself to bless me.

The story I'm about to tell you blesses my heart fresh and new everytime I tell it and I will never forget this beautiful story as long you as He gives me breath. Allow me to share with you a story that seems small but it definitely cheered my heart.

One day, in the summer time, I received word that I would be hitting the road, and the driver was ready to go. Whenever my work makes that statement it basically means there is no time to grab anything, just go. The temperature that day exceeded 90 degrees and the weather channel warned that it was dangerous conditions. I was thirsty, hungry and getting very dizzy because of my lack of food intake that day. I still remember almost passing out, due to the heat and I was praying for a miracle.

We were working on Southfield freeway that day picking up barrels. As I became weaker and weaker, I asked the driver if I could have a minute because dehydration was hitting my body. After a few minutes had passed we continued working and I was trusting God all the way. During that time, McDonalds had something called The Monopoly Game going on where you could win free food. This game was about to prove critical to me, and God was about to bless me in an unusual way. I had no food or money but thankfully I had God.

After about five minutes of work I looked on the ground and saw a McDonald's cup. To my surprise, the cup still had the two Monopoly pieces still on it. As I peeled the pieces off the cup, one of the pieces happened to be a free quarter pounder with cheese. My first thought was this is a one in a million situation and rarely ever do people throw away one of those Monopoly cups without checking the pieces first. It was without a doubt a blessing from God. We went back to work and I had renewed energy that wasn't there before. It was still hot and I was still weak but I was very excited.

As we went down the road a little bit farther God was about to perform a second miracle that day. To my amazement, I looked and found a second McDonalds cup, and that too had the Monopoly pieces on it. I was in total shock at this point. As I peeled off the pieces I found that one of the pieces was a large fry. After our work was over, we went to McDonalds and cashed in my pieces. It was an amazing day and I still stand in awe of what happened. Psalms (E) 115:3 says, "But our God is in the heavens: he hath done whatsoever he hath pleased." Although I will never understand how it came to pass that day, I must conclude that it was God who did it. I will end the chapter with this verse that seems fitting. Psalms (F) 68:19, "Blessed be the Lord, who daily loadeth us with benefits, even the God of our salvation. Selah."

I THESSALONIANS 5:18: *In every thing give thanks: for this is the will of God in Christ Jesus concerning you.*

LUKE 17:12: *And as he entered into a certain village, there met him ten men that were lepers, which stood afar off.*

13: *And they lifted up their voices, and said, Jesus, Master, have mercy on us.*

14: *And when he saw them, he said unto them, Go shew yourselves unto the priests. And it came to pass, that, as they went, they were cleansed.*

15: *And one of them, when he saw that he was healed, turned back, and with a loud voice glorified God.*

16: *And fell down on his face at his feet, giving him thanks: and he was a Samaritan.*

17: *And Jesus answering said, "Were there not ten cleansed? but where are the nine?*

LUKE 17:18: *There are not found that returned to give glory to God, save this stranger.*

19: *And he said unto him, Arise, go thy way: thy faith hath made thee whole.*

2 TIMOTHY 3:2: *For men shall be lovers of their own selves, covetous, boasters, proud, blasphemers, disobedient to parents, unthankful, unholy.*

MATTHEW 24:12: *And because iniquity shall abound, the love of many shall wax cold.*

PSALMS 115:3: *But our God is in the heavens: he hath done whatsoever he hath pleased.*

PSALMS 68:19: *Blessed be the Lord, who daily loadeth us with benefits, even the God of our salvation. Selah.*

TWENTY-SIX
GOD SPEAKING TO A MAN'S HEART BEFORE I COULD, AT WORK

I JOHN 5:16: *If any man see his brother sin a sin which is not unto death, he shall ask, and he shall give him life for them that sin not unto death. There is a sin unto death: I do not say that he shall pray for it.*

THE BIBLE OFTEN TELLS us, in great detail, the dangers of walking away from the Lord and running from His perfect will in our life. Jonah is a good example of someone who tried to flee from the presence of God and found himself in a horrible circumstance. God will never send judgement before He first sends a warning.

Many times, according to the book of Hebrews (A) 12:5-8 God chastens those that are His, but that chastening can reach a point of something more drastic over time. If God's children refuse to repent and get right with God, over a space of time, the bible teaches that God will turn to other forms of punishment. Paul always had a fear, in 1 Corinthians (B) 9:27, of getting away from God and becoming a castaway. In the book of 1 Samuel (C) 18:10 Saul got away from God so bad that God gave him an evil spirit until the day he died. Saul went to heaven, but he was judged for his attitude towards King David.

In Psalms (D) 78:49 we see how God can send people evil angels to afflict and torment those who rebel against His plan for their lives. God punished a man with leprosy, in the Old Testament, for knowingly sinning against the man of God. Whether it is Achan, who stole from God and was stoned, or Samson that had his eyes plucked out by the Philistines, God will use any means necessary to grab one's attention. God is longsuffering and very patient with His children, but there is a time and place where He must send judgement to the back-slider in order to get His divine message across.

The final step, according to Acts chapter 5, 1 John (E) 5:16 and Proverbs (F) 29:1 is a premature death only after all other warnings are unheeded. Many times throughout the bible, and history for that matter, are examples of this divine judgement-taking place in the believer's life. I personally know four times when this has taken place, and every story is very tragic. Revelations (G) 3:16 tells us that the lukewarm Christian makes God sick, and can be spewed (or vomited) out of His mouth. When people leave their first love, and forsake God's will like Demas did in 2 Timothy (H) 4:10, you are surely headed for a whirlwind of destruction.

Please allow me to describe what I'm talking about through a real story that happened, at my work, years ago. This story will open up your eyes to the reality that God is a God of judgement and it should cause you to live more seriously in your walk with the Lord. I'm still in shock that this took place, but it did and I will never forget it. Let me tell you this story and allow the Holy Ghost to minister to your heart in a powerful way.

There was a man, at my work, that I loved as a brother from the first day I met him. Although he had a rough past something about this man was special to me, and I tried my best to help him every chance I got. One day, after witnessing to this man, he fell under deep conviction of God about his sin. For over three nights this man lost sleep, and was shaking in his condition. Joy filled my heart one-day as he attended a Sunday morning service. All the prayers for this man yielded fruit as he walked the aisle and accepted Jesus Christ as his personal Savior. The church shouted the victory and there was a brand new creature standing among us that day. This man instantly volunteered to be baptized and his desire was to help others almost immediately.

For around three months I watched this man serve the Lord and try his absolute best to walk the straight and narrow way for Christ. After three months were over, this man made a common mistake that many Christians make, he started to resort back to bad habits of his past. I watched his life literally being sucked out of him by old friends and old sins that he wasn't willing to forsake. My heart sank as he started drifting away from the Lord and separating himself from me. For months and months he completely left the Lord, and served his flesh. Over and over I would reach out to this man but with no success. I loved him like a brother, and attempted to be a blessing to him, but he ignored all blessings and all warnings that were sent his way. This man became totally entangled in his sin, and was in chains of heaviness that restricted him in serving the Master.

One day, as I drove into work, something very strange took place in my spirit that had never taken place before. From out of nowhere this brother, who I haven't talked with for two months, came to my mind. The Lord would not allow me to get out of the car and begin work until I delivered a certain message to this man. The Lord told me to tell him that if he didn't get right with God, very quickly, danger was headed his way, and God was going to make him a castaway like the bible teaches.

143

I can still remember sitting in my car, for around ten minutes, trying to figure out how I was going to do it. I determined to tell him in private; away from the crowd. As I walked up to the building to deliver this serious message, it was almost like silence filled the air. My soul and spirit was troubled, but I was ready to give this man the bad news. As I walked into the building, to start my workday, a man approached me weeping in a way that was unforgettable. His cheeks were red and sorrow filled his face. In front of everyone, he poured out his heart to me that morning. He told me that God spoke to him and warned him about his spiritual state and he needed to get right with God. He asked me to pray with him, and he told me he would be at church on Sunday. This man seemed very honest and concerned and he kept his word and showed up on Sunday, like he said.

What's amazing about this story is that it wasn't just any man that approached me that day, it was the man who God wanted me to convey the message to. Before I could speak to him, he came searching for me. It's amazing how God deals with His children when we stray away from the fold, but in love and compassion He will leave the ninety and nine and go after that one lost sheep. The great old song, that has touched thousands for Christ, tells the world that "I've wondered far away from God, but now I'm coming home." When you come back to the Father with a broken heart, He will gladly welcome you back with arms wide open, with grace that is able to help in your time of need. Psalms (I) 25:11 says, "For thy name's sake, O LORD, pardon mine iniquity; for it is great." Isaiah (J) 55:7 tells the sinner that if he will forsake his own way, and return unto the Lord, then God will show him mercy and he will abundantly pardon. Thank God we serve a God of love and mercy, and He will always be a God of a second chance to those who will turn to Him.

HEBREWS 12:5: *And she brought forth a man-child, who was to rule all nations with a rod of iron: and her child was caught up unto God, and to his throne.*

6: *And the woman fled into the wilderness, where she hath a place prepared of God, that they should feed her there a thousand two hundred and three-score days.*

7: *And there was war in heaven: Michael and his angels fought against the dragon; and the dragon fought and his angels.*

8: *And prevailed not; neither was their place found any more in heaven.*

1 CORINTHIANS 9:27: *But I keep under my body, and bring it into subjection: lest that by any means, when I have preached to others, I myself should be a castaway.*

1 SAMUEL 18:10: *And Saul sought to smite David even to the wall with the javelin; but he slipped away out of Saul's presence, and he smote the javelin into the wall: and David fled, and escaped that night.*

PSALMS 78:49: *He cast upon them the fierceness of his anger, wrath, and indignation, and trouble, by sending evil angels among them.*

1 JOHN 5:16: *If any man see his brother sin a sin which is not unto death, he shall ask, and he shall give him life for them that sin not unto death. There is a sin unto death: I do not say that he shall pray for it.*

PROVERBS 29:1: *He, that being often reproved hardeneth his neck, shall suddenly be destroyed, and that without remedy.*

REVELATIONS 3:16: *So then because thou art lukewarm, and neither cold nor hot, I will spew thee out of my mouth.*

2 TIMOTHY 4:10: *For Demas hath forsaken me, having loved this present world, and is departed unto Thessalonica; Crescens to Galatia, Titus unto Dalmatia.*

PSALMS 25:1: *For thy name's sake, O LORD, pardon mine iniquity; for it is great.*

ISAIAH 55:7: *Let the wicked forsake his way, and the unrighteous man his thoughts: and let him return unto the LORD, and he will have mercy upon him; and to our God, for he will abundantly pardon.*

TWENTY-SEVEN

FEELING GOD'S POWER AT HOME ONE DAY

LUKE 24:49: *And behold, I send the promise of my Father upon you; but tarry ye in the city of Jerusalem, until ye be endued with power from on high*

WHEN I WAS GROWING up, as a child and even as a young man, I found that the majority of churches I attended frowned upon rejoicing, praising God, saying amen, and of coarse shouting. My mom and dad could tell you that this belief didn't bother me much at the time because in those days I was very quiet and extremely shy. Many times I could go through multiple services without saying anything, but still enjoying the singing and preaching. I did not like attention and would rather be in the shadows in every service I would attend.

The good Lord has always installed in me a deep admiration and respect for God's man, God's people, and God's word. My mom and I have driven five and a half hours, one way, to hear preaching that only lasted one hour while renting a hotel room, and giving that preacher a large love offering to help him along the way.

God knows my heart when I confess to you that I've always struggled with praising the Lord, in the house of God because I do not want to offend people. On the other hand I also do not want to grieve God's Spirit either. Ephesians (A) 4:30 tells us not to grieve His Spirit in church and holding in our praise that God deserves, and holding it back DOES JUST THAT. When you read the book of Psalms you will find hundreds of verses that tell the Christian to praise the Lord for His goodness in the church. Peter said we aught to obey God rather than man. I Thessalonians (B) 4:16 says the Lord shall descend with a shout. Psalms (C) 150:6 says let everything that hath breath praise the Lord. Praise ye the Lord. When Christians refuse to praise the Lord for His blessings, they are grieving the Holy Spirit in the church, and His power can not flow like it could if they would only praise Him.

Over the years God has taught me that praising the Lord, in church, is what God wants you to do. I will praise Him whether others are doing it or not. When I think about how good God has been to me in my life, I can't help but give Him the entire honor He deserves. Everyday of my life, whether it be at church, on the job or even at home, I try to worship the Lord in spirit and in truth. When you love God, others and life your feelings will begin to change concerning shouting and worshiping God. I feel it is a shame that men and women, boys and girls, grandpas and grandmas can go to sporting events and shout till they can't shout anymore, but go to church and just sit there when services are taking place. There is something wrong with that. If we have the victory, then why aren't we excited about it? This once shy boy shouts everywhere he goes and is proud of it.

Let me tell you a true story that took place, in my home one day, a few years back. When I tell you the story think how amazing this is. One day at lunch, God put it on my heart to go home and study in peace for about thirty minutes away from the crowds. When I arrived at my house it was indeed peaceful as my condominium looked like a ghost town. I remember sitting down and opening my bible to Ephesians chapter 3 and reading that great chapter. When I arrived at verse 19 and 20 of that chapter, God got a hold of my heart in a powerful way. I read the phrase, "that ye might be filled with all the fullness of God," and something turned on in my soul.

The glory of God filled my house and before I knew it I was shouting in praise to the Lord. I called my boss and when he answered I shouted at the top of my lungs for the joy that was in my heart. The impact of that shout was so powerful that an object, in my house, fell over from about 10 feet away. He asked if I had neighbors and I said, "Yes." He said if they were sleeping they are awake now. After we ended our conversation I stood up the object that had fell over and thanked God for his power and blessings on my life. Jesus said in Matthew (D) 5:16 let your light shine before men, and that's what we all should try to do. The bible says that the Lord hath done great things for us; whereof we are glad.

EPHESIANS 4:30: *And grieve not the Holy Spirit of God, whereby ye are sealed unto the day of redemption.*

I THESSALONIANS 4:16: *For the Lord himself shall descend from heaven with a shout, with the voice of the archangel, and with the trump of God: and the dead in Christ shall rise first.*

PSALMS 150:6: *Let every thing that hath breath praise the LORD. Praise ye the LORD.*

MATTHEW 5:16: *Let your light so shine before men, that they may see your good works, and glorify your Father which is in heaven.*

TWENTY-EIGHT
FEELING GOD'S POWER AT WORK

PHILIPPIANS 3:10: *that I may know Him and the power of His resurrection*

MANY TIMES, OVER THE years at work, I have felt an overflowing of God's power. Many miracles have been seen, many have been saved, and all have heard about the Lord. My co-workers are precious to me and I love them with all my heart. Many of them are like family and I would go to any extreme to help them.

Often, through the years, I have shouted for joy, sang hymns in their presence, and talked about Jesus whenever a door opens for me. Sometimes I feel like I'm the only hope they have and I must point them to Jesus. I'm not afraid to stand up for the Lord, and I'm definitely not afraid to praise His Holy name.

For many years I worked by myself and others would hear me shout from far distances away. One day I was in the yard by myself and it was one of the coldest days of winter. While people were getting warm inside, my heart was being warmed outside as I was thinking about the love of God. As

I remember correctly God's Spirit overshadowed me one day and I lifted up my voice in praise to the Father. When I shouted I was about 1,300 feet from the building and the bay door was closed. In just a moment I looked and the bay door was opening and sure enough here comes the boss on the golf cart. When he finally came to where I was he asked me if everything was all right. I said, "Life couldn't be better, sir." He heard me all the way in the building through the big bay door.

There have been times, at work, when His glory fell upon me and I would work as if I was five people instead of one. God would empower, strengthen, and use me for His honor and praise. Without His Spirit working in our souls we would live defeated lives but thanks be to God that giveth us the victory (I Corinthians (A) 15:57). Many amazing stories can be told about encounters from God at my work but let me tell you one that sticks out concerning praising the Lord.

One day, at my work, as I was putting an order together with another co-worker, God filled me with His Spirit. This moving of God promoted me to shout like never before. It seemed like time stood still for a second as praise left my lips. I still remember going back to work as though nothing ever happened. Over the span of about forty minutes nature took its course and I had to use the restroom. When I made it to the building it felt like every radio was blaring at a very high level. As I walked through the shop I noticed that a man named Ed Harris was smiling at me. I asked him, why he was smiling at me? He gave me a response that I really couldn't believe. He said I'm smiling because I heard you from inside the shop over these radios that are playing and I just shook my head and smiled. There were five radios playing, machines running, and other noises going on at the same time. When I shouted to the Lord, I was around 1,200 feet from the building and all the doors were shut. Psalms (B) 93:4 says that the Lord on high is mightier than the noise of many waters, yea than the mighty waves of the sea. When we lift up our voices unto Him, God will be pleased, and we will be blessed.

I CORINTHIANS 15:57: *But thanks be to God, which giveth us the victory through our Lord Jesus Christ.*

PSALMS 93:4: *The LORD on high is mightier than the noise of many waters, yea, than the mighty waves of the sea.*

TWENTY-NINE

FEELING GOD'S POWER AT CHURCH

LUKE 17:15: *And one of them, when he saw that he was healed, turned back, and with a loud voice glorified God.*

MY WIFE AND I made plans one weekend to take a three-day vacation and travel up to her grandmothers's house in Hillsdale, Michigan. I was very weary, fatigued and physically drained due to work, church, and the pressures of life. Over the years I have learned that sometimes it is good to come apart and rest a while like Jesus told His disciples. When my wife and I travel to Hillsdale, we always make it a habit to visit a friend of ours that Pastor's in Jonesville, Michigan and try to encourage him in some way. The Pastors name is Tom McCue and his church is Fellowship Baptist Church.

Pastor McCue is one of my ten favorite preachers, and he is unique in every way. He stands six foot seven inches tall and weighs about four hundred pounds. He has bad feet but preaches with power from on high. Whenever I am blessed, to hear Pastor McCue preach the word of God it always encourages my heart and ignites my soul. The story I'm about to tell happened at Pastor McCue's church and it will never lose its power, in my heart, and Lord willing in your heart as well. In all my years in church I have never seen a story like this before and I may never see one like it again. Let me tell you this story and allow God to speak to your heart.

One Sunday morning, my family and I attended Fellowship Baptist Church in hopes of being a blessing to the man of God, and his ministry. We were greeted with friendly handshakes and warm words as we took our seat in the front. The crowd was pretty small that day, the service had no energy, and seemingly no life during the song service. When Pastor McCue mounted the pulpit he welcomed the visitors and opened to the book of Joshua. Joy bells were ringing in my soul as Pastor McCue began his sermon.

As I normally do, when preaching is being brought forth, I shouted "AMEN" in praise and thankfulness for God's word being thundered by God's man. As the sermon went longer and longer, I realized that I was the only person in the whole church that was supporting the Pastor and his message. His members failed to notice that their leader was pouring his heart out that day with little or no appreciation in return.

After the service was over my heart was heavy for the man of God. As I went back to my wife's grandmother's house I felt for my friend and thought about him for much of the afternoon. I decided to return to Fellowship Baptist for the evening service to hear the Assistant Pastor preach. As I was shaking hands, something happened that stunned me. In the middle of talking to a very nice lady, from that church, an elderly lady was determined to give me a piece of her mind. This elderly lady was probably in her eighties and struggled to even make it to her seat. She looked me right in my eyes and without hesitation said, "Young man, when you shout and carry on that really annoys me, and I wish you would stop." Her statement was very direct and very bold. I responded by saying, "I'm sorry if I offended you, but the scriptures are full of verses where God encourages us to shout and I am just trying to help God's man."

As the young preacher stood up to preach I tried my best to ignore what had just happened. However, her words kept ringing in my ears all night long. In my heart I knew if she did not repent quickly for what she said to me, trouble was headed her way. The preacher preached a wonderful message that night that spoke to hearts within the congregation. When the invitation was given I went to the altar to thank God for the message I heard that night and for His goodness towards me. As I was praying something happened that totally surprised me. That elderly lady that could hardly move ran to the altar like an Olympic sprinter and begged for forgiveness because of her rude words towards me. That was the first time, in my life, I have ever seen a lady of her age admit she was wrong and apologize to someone of my age.

God's fear gripped her heart that night as she cried out to God. She sought me out after the service and asked me to forgive her for what she did. God's Spirit was grieved that day but thank God she got things right. I still wonder what would have happened if she would not have repented that day. This story reminds me of that old song we teach our kids in Sunday school while they are young entitled, "Oh be careful little mouth what you say." As I drove back home that night I was reminded of the awesome judgement of an Almighty God. The next time you see someone praising God, you may want to think before you speak.

THIRTY
GOD CAN BE CLEARLY SEEN WHEN YOU CHOOSE TO LOOK FOR HIM

LUKE 2:30: *For mine eyes have seen thy salvation.*

IN THIS WORLD WE live in today many people claim that they are atheists, and that God is not real. They will go to great extremes to deny the bible, and instead go about to establish their own righteousness. They reject that the bible is inspired and they have no faith in a supernatural God that spoke the world into existence. To argue with this type of person is pointless, and the bible teaches that they are willingly ignorant (2 Peter (A) 3:5).

The word of God teaches, in Romans (B) 1:20 for the invisible things of him from the creation of the world are clearly seen, being understood by the things that are made, even his eternal power and Godhead; so that they are without excuse. Hebrews (C) 11:1 says, "Now faith is the substance of things hoped for, the evidence of things not seen." In other words, God teaches us, through His word, that in every person's life there are certain times and places when God reveals His truth to mankind.

158

Salvation of the soul, according to Jonah, is of the Lord, and it comes and goes like the wind; found in John (D) 3:8. God will enlighten a man or woman's pathway in a fashion that is real and eye opening. During these rare and special encounters mankind is forced to make a spiritual decision that will change their future, forever. According to Isaiah (E) 55:6 we must do it on God's timetable, not our timetable. This decision, that you must make, could either be the greatest of your life or the worst of your life.

Many people make the decision to reject the Light, and as a result they forever abide in the dark. Romans (F) 1:21 teaches, "Because that, when they knew God, they glorified him not as God, neither were thankful; but became vain in their imaginations, and their foolish heart was darkened." Once darkness overtakes a person and they refuse the Savior, God, according to Romans (G) 1:28 refuses them and gives them something called a reprobate mind. Once this process takes place in a person's heart and mind there is no hope of reaching that person with the glorious Light again. The next step, in their lives, is total foolishness, wickedness, unrighteousness, disobedience, inventors of evil things, corrupt minds, proud, boasters, haters of God and so on and so forth. When you accept the Lord, and become a child of the King, everything is clearly seen. On the other hand when you refuse the Light, everything is blurry and impossible for you to see.

Titus (H) 1:15 teaches that, "Unto the pure all things are pure: but unto them that are defiled and unbelieving is nothing pure; but even their mind and conscience is defiled." Once, God makes you a reprobate and turns you over to Satan, your understanding of spiritual matters will be eternally gone. In 2 Corinthians (I) 4:3 the Bible says, "but if our gospel be hid, it is hid to them that are lost," verse 4 "In whom the god of this world hath blinded the minds of them, which believe not, lest the light of the glorious gospel of Christ, who is the image of God, should shine unto them. Those verses say the Gospel is hid to them that are lost. God's word tells us that the God of this world hath blinded the minds of them, which believe not. 1 Timothy (J) 4:2 says, "Speaking lies in hypocrisy; having their conscience seared with a hot iron." The scriptures say, God sears people's consciences with a hot iron. In other words, it's not a question if God is real, but it is a question of what you have done with the Light that God has already tried to give you.

Jesus said, "I am the light of the world: he that followeth me shall not walk in darkness, but shall have the Light of Life." (John: (K) 8:12) 1 John (L) 1:7 says, "But if we walk in the light, as he is in the light, we have fellowship one with another, and the blood of Jesus Christ his Son cleanseth us from all sin." God is the only one, in this world, that has the power to give Light to a fallen sinner and raise them from a dead state according to Ephesians (M) 2:1. Even though a sinner takes this spiritual calling for granted, God takes it very seriously. Jesus said, in John (N) 12:35, yet a little while is the light with you. Walk while ye have the light, lest darkness come upon you: for he that walketh in darkness knoweth not whither he goeth.

The bible says in Romans (O) 3:4 God forbid: yea, let God be true, but every man a liar; as it is written, that thou mightest be justified in thy sayings, and mightest overcome when thou art judged. Psalms (P) 19:7 the law of the LORD is perfect, converting the soul: the testimony of the LORD is sure, making wise the simple. Matthew (Q) 24:35: Heaven and earth shall pass away, but my words shall not pass away. May I submit to you that people that claim they are atheists are people who rejected Christ at some point in their lives and God rejected them. God's word is perfect but man's opinions are wrong. According to God's Holy word, the book of Titus (R) 2:11 says, *For the grace of God that bringeth salvation hath appeared to all men.*

That includes all of those who claim to be atheists. Either God is lying when he said that His grace has appeared to all men, or the atheist is lying!

The bible says in Titus (S) 1:2 "In hope of eternal life, which God, that cannot lie, promised before the world began." Hebrews (T) 6:18 says,"That by two immutable things, in which it was impossible for God to lie, we might have a strong consolation, who have fled for refuge to lay hold upon the hope set before us." However, in the book of Psalms (U) 116:11 the bible says, "I said in my haste, All men are liars." God is a God of truth and righteousness and His word teaches in Psalms (V) 8:4: What is man, that thou art mindful of him? And the son of man, that thou visitest him?

Atheists ignore obvious proofs that God is real, on a daily basis, and allow the Devil to blind their eyes, while truth passes them by. Everytime the sun rises in the morning and the moon shines at night, God is reminding us that He exists, found in Psalms (W) 19:1-2. Everytime a baby is born, something in our spirit reminds us there is a God found in Psalms (X) 139:13-18. Everytime a rainbow appears in the sky, God reminds us that there is a God according to Genesis (Y) 9:12-16. Everytime a volcano erupts it reminds mankind that there is a fire in hell found in Job (Z) 28:5. Everywhere we turn and anywhere we look the footprints of the Nazarene can clearly be seen. For the rest of this chapter I am going to give you examples that will prove to you the realness of God from my own personal experiences. Although I will only list a few examples to prove to you God is real, the truth is I could give you many more but time will not allow me. I hope you enjoy these powerful and timely experiences that I have had and I pray they will change your mind forever.

The bible teaches us in Psalms (AA) 118:24: This is the day which the LORD hath made; we will rejoice and be glad in it. Everyday of my life I realize that each day is different than the next, and God has something new for me if I will only look for it. As I work, shop, travel or worship my eyes are always searching for something from the Lord that is fresh and new. We that understand Psalms (BB) 139:7-10, know that everywhere we go in life God goes with us. Sometimes we miss His presence and things He sends our way because our minds are occupied with everything else. A good example of this would be a sign that I see often while driving down the road working construction. The sign simply says, "Prepare to meet thy God Amos" (CC) 4:12: It seems like everytime we drive by that sign it jumps out at me, and it speaks to me. With that being said, there are thousands that will pass that same sign, in their own travels each day, and will fail to notice that it even exists.

God's presence surrounds mankind and can easily be seen if we will only look for it. Isaiah (DD) 45:22. Look unto me, and be ye saved, all the ends of the earth: for I am God, and there is none else. Sometimes God sends things our way when we are hurting to remind us that He loves us. Psalms (EE) 147:5, "Great is our Lord, and of great power: his understanding is infinite." Many times when we feel at our lowest state in life, God shows up to encourage us to go another mile for Him.

I can still remember a few years ago when God showed up, in a special way for my family, in a tough time in our lives. My Grandfather just died and he was very dear to us. It is never easy losing a loved one, but it makes it much better when you know they are in heaven upon leaving this life. Many people gave testimonies about his life at the funeral, and most wept while doing so. We sang his favorite hymns, and preached to my family that day. We could definitely feel God's spirit that day and it was hard to say goodbye.

After the services were concluded I felt the need to ride with my mom over to the cemetery and offer support in anyway

I could. We talked for a minute and shared verses with one another as my dad drove. About five minutes into our drive I told my mom to look over to her left, for God had a message for her that day. As my mom looked to her left there was a sign that said, "I am the Resurrection and the Life. It reminded us of the fact that even though we were burying her dad, and my grandfather, we would see him again through Jesus and the power of His resurrection. God has a way of showing up when you need Him most. There have been times, in my walk with God, when His presence has been so strong that others around me could not deny it either. Many times at church, at home, at work, or on the road, silence has overshadowed the area, and God has showed up when we least expected it.

This last example I want to give you will change your life, if you will allow the Holy Spirit to speak to your heart. This example is powerful and revealing, and is stunning in every single way. Allow me to tell you a true story that happened while driving with a man at my work.

One day, at around 1:30 p.m., my boss notified me that I was going on a long ride and I would not be back until late that night. I grabbed my lunch and headed out on the ride with a man whom I have so much respect for. This man always treats me well and we help each other nearly everyday. This man is not a Christian, but he has values and respects those who are Christians. I remember going on a two-hour drive that day and finding myself in an area that was secluded and barren. It seemed like we kept driving deeper and deeper into the woods, and human life was nowhere to be found. As we were talking his phone rang and the man answered and got some bad news. He found out that his father-in-law had passed away. He became very sad. He told me the news and my heart broke for him. I tried to comfort him the best I could.

God opened a door for me that day and we began to talk about life and death and the importance of knowing Christ before we die. As we began to talk about death, the Spirit of God told me to point to a tree in the middle of nowhere. Believe it or not, there was a sign on the tree that had the famous verse that says, "For the wages of sin is death; but the gift of God is eternal life through Jesus Christ our Lord."(Romans (FF) 6:23) The timing was perfect and silence filled the truck for over a minute, as we were speechless.

God showed up in the backwoods that day and His presence was real. Around two months later I was with the same man, but this time in Detroit, Michigan. As we were driving, the subject about heaven and hell came up again. God's Spirit started to move in that truck. I shared some verses with him and told him how much God loved him. After a few minutes the conversation got serious, and I made a statement that we will never forget. I remember looking at the man and telling him that one verse of scripture applies to his life, more than any other, in the entire bible. He asked me what verse I was referring to. I told him that the verse I was thinking about was Hebrews (GG) 9:27. After I told him that verse the conversation ended and for about five minutes nothing was said. I can remember, as we were arriving at our destination, I happened to look to my right and I couldn't believe my eyes. I asked the man to read what the sign said that I was looking at. He said the sign says, "Hebrews (GG) 9:27 And as it is appointed unto men once to die, but after this the judgment." Again silence filled that truck because he and I both knew that God was real that day.

When you wake up to the reality that God is real, your eyes will begin to see things that they have never seen before. The bible says in Psalms (HH) 14:1: The fool hath said in his heart, there is no God, they are corrupt, they have done abominable works, there is none that doeth good. I pray that through this chapter it has dawned on you that God really does exist and He ever liveth to make intercession for us (Romans (II) 8:26). The scriptures also says, in 2 Peter (JJ) 3:9 The Lord is not slack concerning his promise, as some men count slackness; but is longsuffering to us-ward, not willing that any should perish, but that all should come to repentance. Come to Christ today and find out what life is all about.

2 PETER 3:5: *For this they willingly are ignorant of, that by the word of God the heavens were of old, and the earth standing out of the water and in the water.*

ROMANS 1:20: *For the invisible things of him from the creation of the world are clearly seen, being understood by the things that are made, even his eternal power and Godhead; so that they are without excuse.*

HEBREWS 11:1: *Now faith is the substance of things hoped for, the evidence of things not seen.*

JOHN 3:8: *The wind bloweth where it listeth, and thou hearest the sound thereof, but canst not tell whence it cometh, and whither it goeth: so is every one that is born of the Spirit.*

ISAIAH 55:6: *Seek ye the LORD while he may be found, call ye upon him while he is near.*

ROMANS 1:21: *Because that, when they knew God, they glorified him not as God, neither were thankful; but became vain in their imaginations, and their foolish heart was darkened.*

ROMANS 1:28: *And even as they did not like to retain God in their knowledge, God gave them over to a reprobate mind, to do those things which are not convenient.*

TITUS 1:15: *Unto the pure all things are pure: but unto them that are defiled and unbelieving is nothing pure; but even their mind and conscience is defiled.*

2 CORINTHIANS 4:3: *But if our gospel be hid, it is hid to them that are lost:4: In whom the god of this world hath blinded the minds of them which believe not, lest the light of the glorious gospel of Christ, who is the image of God, should shine unto them. It says the Gospel is hid to them that are lost.*

1 TIMOTHY 4:2: *Speaking lies in hypocrisy; having their conscience seared with a hot iron; says God sears peoples consciences with a hot iron.*

JOHN: 8:12: *Then spake Jesus again unto them, saying, I am the light of the world: he that followeth me shall not walk in darkness, but shall have the light of life.*

1 JOHN 1:7: *But if we walk in the light, as he is in the light, we have fellowship one with another, and the blood of Jesus Christ his Son cleanseth us from all sin.*

EPHESIANS 2:1: *And you hath he quickened, who were dead in trespasses and sins.*

JOHN 12:35: *Then Jesus said unto them, Yet a little while is the light with you. Walk while ye have the light, lest darkness come upon you: for he that walketh in darkness knoweth not whither he goeth.*

ROMANS 3:4: *God forbid: yea, let God be true, but every man a liar; as it is written, That thou mightest be justified in thy sayings, and mightest overcome when thou art judged.*

PSALMS 19:7: *The law of the LORD is perfect, converting the soul: the testimony of the LORD is sure, making wise the simple.*

MATTHEW 24:35: *Heaven and earth shall pass away, but my words shall not pass away.*

TITUS 2:11: *For the grace of God that bringeth salvation hath appeared to all men.*

TITUS 1:2: *In hope of eternal life, which God, that cannot lie, promised before the world began.*

HEBREWS 6:18: *That by two immutable things, in which it was impossible for God to lie, we might have a strong consolation, who have fled for refuge to lay hold upon the hope set before us.*

PSALMS 116:11: *I said in my haste, All men are liars.*

PSALMS 8:4: *What is man, that thou art mindful of him? and the son of man, that thou visitest him?*

PSALMS 19:1: *The heavens declare the glory of God; and the firmament sheweth his handywork.*

2: *Day unto day uttereth speech, and night unto night sheweth knowledge.*

PSALMS 139:13: *For thou hast possessed my reins: thou hast covered me in my mother's womb.*

PSALMS 139:14: *I will praise thee; for I am fearfully and wonderfully made: marvellous are thy works; and that my soul knoweth right well.*

15: *My substance was not hid from thee, when I was made in secret, and curiously wrought in the lowest parts of the earth.*

16: *Thine eyes did see my substance, yet being unperfect; and in thy book all my members were written, which in continuance were fashioned, when as yet there was none of them.*

17: *How precious also are thy thoughts unto me, O God! how great is the sum of them!*

18: *If I should count them, they are more in number than the sand: when I awake, I am still with thee.*

GENESIS 9:12: *And God said, This is the token of the covenant which I make between me and you and every living creature that is with you, for perpetual generations.*

GENESIS 9:13: *I do set my bow in the cloud, and it shall be for a token of a covenant between me and the earth.*

14: *And it shall come to pass, when I bring a cloud over the earth, that the bow shall be seen in the cloud.*

15: *And I will remember my covenant, which is between me and you and every living creature of all flesh; and the waters shall no more become a flood to destroy all flesh.*

16: *And the bow shall be in the cloud; and I will look upon it, that I may remember the everlasting covenant between God and every living creature of all flesh that is upon the earth.*

JOB 28:5: *As for the earth, out of it cometh bread: and under it is turned up as it were fire.*

PSALMS (AA) 118:24: *This is the day which the LORD hath made; we will rejoice and be glad in it.*

PSALMS (BB) 139:7: *Whither shall I go from thy spirit? or whither shall I flee from thy presence?*

8: *If I ascend up into heaven, thou art there: if I make my bed in hell, behold, thou art there.*

9: *If I take the wings of the morning, and dwell in the uttermost parts of the sea.*

10: *Even there shall thy hand lead me, and thy right hand shall hold me.*

AMOS 4:12: *Therefore thus will I do unto thee, O Israel: and because I will do this unto thee, prepare to meet thy God, O Israel.*

ISAIAH (DD) 45:22: *Look unto me, and be ye saved, all the ends of the earth: for I am God, and there is none else.*

PSALMS (EE) 147:5: *Great is our Lord, and of great power: his understanding is infinite.*

ROMANS 6:23: *For the wages of sin is death; but the gift of God is eternal life through Jesus Christ our Lord.*

HEBREWS 9:27: *And as it is appointed unto men once to die, but after this the judgment:*

PSALMS 14:1: *The fool hath said in his heart, There is no God. They are corrupt, they have done abominable works, there is none that doeth good.*

ROMANS 8:26: *Likewise the Spirit also helpeth our infirmities: for we know not what we should pray for as we ought: but the Spirit itself maketh intercession for us with groanings which cannot be uttered.*

2 PETER 3:9: *The Lord is not slack concerning his promise, as some men count slackness; but is long-suffering to us-ward, not willing that any should perish, but that all should come to repentance.*

CONCLUSION

ECCLESIASTES 12:13: *Let us hear the conclusion of the whole matter: Fear God, and keep his commandments: for this is the whole duty of man.*

IN MY CLOSING STATEMENT, let me begin by thanking each and every person who was kind enough to purchase a copy of this book. You are all very special to me and I pray that this book blessed your hearts. Without your love and support where would authors be. Thanks for going on this journey with me. I really appreciate it from the bottom of my heart. Sometimes, in life, we tend to doubt if God cares for us and we begin to question if He is still able to show up in our times of desperation. We allow the devil to play with our minds and before we know it our lives are shipwrecked and destroyed. May I caution you never to entertain negative thoughts that take you away from the abundant life that is in Christ Jesus our Lord. Always think positive and understand that God is in control and we will be the winners, someday. The bible declares in I Corinthians (A) 15:57 that thanks be to God, which giveth us the victory through our Lord Jesus Christ. This book proves that God is still able to perform miracles today just like He did in days gone by. Stop doubting the Lord and start believing that He can still do the impossible. Matthew (B) 19:26 tells us that with men this is impossible; but with God all things are possible. We serve a God that can move in a mighty way and can still work wonders in the sight of men. The bible says in Matthew(C) 21:22 that all things whatsoever ye shall ask in prayer, believing, ye shall receive.

I pray this book has spoken to your heart and has caused you to think about the Lord in a whole different light. My prayer is that God's saints have gained strength, hope, and assurance through this publication. I also pray that the lost have gained a respect, fear, and longing in their soul that was not there before. In John (D) 6:37 the bible says, "To Him that cometh unto Me, I will no wise cast out. John (E) 3:16 says, For God so loved the world, that He gave His only begotten Son, that whosoever believeth in Him should not perish but have everlasting life. Jesus has offered a priceless gift that costs us nothing, but it cost Him everything. Turn to Jesus today and discover a love like you have never known. May God bless you, and I want you to know that I love you.

I feel, in my heart, that the best way to conclude this project is to direct you to a verse that puts the final stamp on this book. David said, in Psalms (F) 41:13, "Blessed be the LORD God of Israel from everlasting, and to everlasting. Amen, and Amen." May we never depend on our own strength but always on the strength of the Almighty. Like the old hymn says, "On Christ the solid Rock I stand, all other ground is sinking sand. All other ground is sinking sand."

With Love,
Brother Tony

I CORINTHIANS 15:57: *But thanks be to God, which giveth us the victory through our Lord Jesus Christ.*

MATTHEW 19:26: *But Jesus beheld them, and said unto them, With men this is impossible; but with God all things are possible.*

MATTHEW 21:22: *And all things, whatsoever ye shall ask in prayer, believing, ye shall receive.*

JOHN 6:37: *All that the Father giveth me shall come to me; and him that cometh to me I will in no wise cast out.*

JOHN 3:16: *For God so loved the world, that he gave his only begotten Son, that whosoever believeth in him should not perish, but have everlasting life.*

PSALMS 41:13: *Blessed be the LORD God of Israel from everlasting, and to everlasting. Amen, and Amen.*

ABOUT THE AUTHOR

My name is Anthony James Ritthaler, but most people call me "Bro Tony." I was raised in a great church by my godly parents during my childhood. All throughout my life God has protected, sheltered and guided me in ways that are staggering, to say the least. In 2009, God allowed me to marry my wife Erin and a year later we welcomed the birth of our first child Hope.

The Lord has showered down His blessings upon me in many forms and fashions through the years. My hobbies include sports, studding, history and reading God's Word. I live in Canton, Michigan and attend Hope Baptist Church in Huron Township. My occupation is road construction and I have done this for eleven years. God has used me through the years to help God's men and for that I am very grateful. You will find out more as you study this book, and I pray it will minister to your heart.